COLLECTED POEMS

Fiction

*Saturday Night and Sunday
     Morning*
*The Loneliness of the Long Distance
     Runner*
The General
Key to the Door
The Ragman's Daughter
The Death of William Posters
A Tree on Fire
Guzman, Go Home
A Start in Life
Travels in Nihilon
Raw Material
Men, Women and Children
The Flame of Life
The Widower's Son
The Storyteller
*The Second Chance and Other
     Stories*
Her Victory
The Lost Flying Boat
Down From the Hill
Life Goes On
Out of the Whirlpool
The Open Door
Last Loves
Leonard's War
Snowstop

Poetry

The Rats and Other Poems
*A Falling Out of Love and Other
     Poems*
*Love in the Environs of Voronezh
     and Other Poems*
Storm and Other Poems
Snow on the North Side of Lucifer
Sun Before Departure
Tides and Stone Walls

Plays

All Citizens are Soldiers (with Ruth
     Fainlight)
Three Plays

Essays

Mountains and Caverns

For Children

*The City Adventures of Marmalade
     Jim*
Big John and the Stars
The Incredible Fencing Fleas
Marmalade Jim on the Farm
Marmalade Jim and the Fox

ALAN SILLITOE

COLLECTED POEMS

 HarperCollins*Publishers*

HarperCollins*Publishers*
77–85 Fulham Palace Road,
Hammersmith, London W6 8JB

Published by HarperCollins*Publishers* 1993
9 8 7 6 5 4 3 2 1

Some of the poems were previously published and are taken from
the following titles: *The Rats and Other Poems, A Falling Out of
Love and Other Poems, Love in the Environs of Voronezh and Other
Poems, Storm and Other Poems, Snow on the North Side of Lucifer,
Sun Before Departure, Tides and Stone Walls.*

A catalogue record for this book is
available from the British Library

ISBN 0 00 223928 0

Set in Linotron Galliard by
Rowland Phototypesetting Ltd
Bury St Edmunds, Suffolk

Printed in Great Britain by
HarperCollinsManufacturing Glasgow

CONTENTS

from Love in the Environs of Voronezh and Other Poems *and* Storm and Other Poems, 1968 and 1974

from Snow on the North Side of Lucifer, 1979

from Sun Before Departure, 1974 –1982

PREFACE

Unlike a novelist, who may hide behind his fiction for the whole of his writing life, a poet who presents his collected poems displays the emotional history of his heart and soul. Such a record, however seemingly disguised, cannot be falsified, supposing of course that the poems are true to himself, and what poems are not, if they are poems? That is the condition which I have followed in assembling this collection: the assumption that the inner life is more discernible, though perhaps only after diligent searching, than any self-portrayal in a story or novel.

From seven short volumes written between 1950 and 1990 I have chosen less than half the verse published, and therefore ask myself whether, if the omitted matter were put into another book, would it present a different picture of the state of the heart and soul over the same period? That may be a novelist's question, but the answer is a fair 'no', for the material left out was mostly the fat and gristle surrounding the meat of what is printed here.

I was surprised at times by the extreme revision most of the poems so obviously needed when, all those years ago, I had considered them indisputably finished. Even so, I can't imagine that in the years to come I shall see any cause to amend them again. Though I shall no doubt look into the book from time to time, I shall no more be tempted to re-write than I am when looking into a previously published novel. Only in that way do the novelist and the poet coincide in me, otherwise the two entities are so separate that we might be two different people. Why this is I shall never know, unless there are some things which can never be said in fiction. They simply don't fit, being drawn from an elevation of the psyche which the novel can know nothing about.

When I became a writer it was as a poet, but it didn't take

long for fiction to obtrude, perhaps to fill in those spaces which must necessarily exist between one poem and another, my temperament having decided that during my life I could not be permitted to be unoccupied for a moment. Such periods of emptiness, being too fearful to contemplate, were duly filled, and have been so ever since. The unconscious fear of idleness prevents me from brooding too heavily on my fate except in such a way that produces stories and novels.

The earliest poems in *The Rats* volume came while I was working on *Saturday Night and Sunday Morning*, but all the other poems were written during the progress of various novels. The sentiments deployed in *The Rats* bled into the views of the hero of my first novel, but from that point on, poetry and fiction came out of totally different territories. A later volume, *Tides and Stone Walls*, was written to a series of remarkable photographs by Victor Bowley, and the poems chosen from that book are those which in my view rely on the photographs least, though even then they were directly inspired by them. Twenty-one more recent poems at the end of the present book are 'new' in that they have not been previously collected.

The Rats and Other Poems was written by an exile returning to England who, having spent a total of eight years out of the country before the age of thirty, expected to go away again to write in an isolation which he had found congenial. It did not happen, but it has always seemed to me that a poet and writer, wherever he lives, even if on home territory, suffers exile for life. Geography notwithstanding, such displacement is a kind of mental stand-off from the rest of society, giving the detachment to see the surroundings with a calculating eye – not an emotionally cold eye, but one which uses language and observation from a standpoint entirely personal.

ALAN SILLITOE

from The Rats and Other Poems, 1960

SHADOW

When on a familiar but deserted beach
You meet a gentleman you recognize
As your own death, know who he is and teach
Yourself he comes with flower-blue eyes

To wipe the salt-spray from all new intentions,
And kiss you on each sunken cheek to ease
Into your blood the strength to leave this life:
(A minor transmutation of disease)

To watch the mechanism of each arm
Inside your arms of flesh and fingernail,
To despise the ancient wild alarm
Behind each eye. Shaking your hand so frail

Your own death breathes possessive fire
(A familiar voice that no one understands)
Striding quickly, sporting elegant attire,
Coming towards you on these once deserted sands.

POEM WRITTEN
IN MAJORCA

Death has no power in these clear skies
Where olives in December shed their milk:
Too temperate to strike
At orange-terraces and archaic moon:

But Death is strong where hemlock stones
Stand at the foot of cold Druidic hills;
There I was born when snow lay
Under naked willows, and frost
Boomed along grey ponds at afternoon,
Frightening birds that
Though hardened for long winters,
Fled from the nerve-filled ground,
Beat their soundless wings away
From Death's first inflicted wound.

RUTH'S FIRST SWIM IN THE MEDITERRANEAN, 1952

The water that touches your thighs
Swallowed the STRUMA.
Water that folded the wings of Icarus
Climbs your limbs, sharp with salt
That stiffened the beard of Odysseus.
Tragedy, comedy, legend and history –
Invisible wakes through centuries
Of exiles seeking home:
You turn and look as if at
The wandering Ark of the Hebrews,
Then cleave the waters of your Inland Sea.

You had a dream last night:
Deep in my primeval sleep
A match was made between my heart and yours
And I moved into love with you
And found your body willing.

Maybe it began with you
When deep in your primeval sleep
A wielding of desire for some
Fulfilling (too matter of fact
And clumsy in afternoon or evening)
Drew me out of some too private dream
And held us plough to furrow.

No judgement made, for neither side
Can settle on the cause,
And no more thought is here but this:
What if a birth should come
Out of our midnight dreams?

TO RUTH

If I throw out my arms and strike
The night that comes, open my heart
To whoever guards survivors, favours struggles
Carries sunshine garlanded about
Her waist, will my fight fail?
Will I unbuckle my resistance
In the darkness? Let ice melt
Fear kill, suffer death to take me?

Though passion is not greatness
Nor greatness passion
When measured by such fluid odds
As sunlight and death,
Passion augments
The alchemy of returning life
Stands the blood high in its demand,
Becomes supremely knowing,
And draws me back
Into the living battle of our love.

OUT OF
MY THOUSAND VOICES

Out of my thousand voices
I speak with one
To the waves and flying saltfoam,
Flinging the dovetailed words
Of a single voice
At the knife-edged prow
Of the ship unbreakable
That carries her away.

I throw the one remaining voice
Of all my thousand out to sea
And watch it curving
Into the black-paunched water
Like a falling star,
A single word of love
That drops into the grave,
A thousand echoes falling by her ship.

ISLANDS

One great problem poses:
What is that island we're passing?
Green hills, white houses,
Grey peak, a blue sky,
Ship sailing smooth.

These problems arise
On islands that pass,
White houses lived in
And mountains climbed,
Clouds moving like ships
And ships like clouds.

We on deck open baskets for lunch
To feed the problem of each white island
Of how steep such contours
And shallow those bays,
And who keens that song
In pinewoods by the shore.
'How beautiful it is' –
And how remote, waiting for other islands
We shall pass, puzzled that the birds
Can dip their wings at many.

What is that island we're passing
Heartshaped and hemlocked
Watered by a winding stream?
A monument to us and we a monument to it —
A great problem posed
Till each unanswering island
Left in darkness grows a separate light:
Solutions beyond reach:
Cobalt funereal in the deep sea.

ICARUS

The ocean was timeless, blue
When your unwaxed wings wheeled towards heaven.
Wind was recalled, emptiness new
And smooth as Thermopylae's lagoon given

To the Heroes' barge held in repose. Nothing stirred:
The gods watched and held their breath
Forgot to stake each others' wives, heard
Wings feather the air, dip and climb. Death

Did not come to Daedalus. The sun
Heliographed his escaper, watched his prison cloak
Colouring the sea, shadowing his one
Track channelled to Italy, whose mirror spoke

For his safety. Icarus found entirety
In a gleam from the sun. Was it a lotus-land
He climbed to? A mission of piety
Foretelling a lesser doom written upon sand

For older men? Or pure myth? His wings aileroned
The windless air and carried him in a curve
Measured by a rainbow's greatness above the honed
Earth: lifted him through a mauve

Loophole of sky. No ships sleeved
The water and filled a farewell in their sails
Or circled the fallen wings, or grieved,
And Daedalus, onward flying, knew no warning fairytales.

11

CARTHAGE

Scorpions lurk under loose stones
Marked on Leipzig maps, and electric tramways
Ride shallow loops over thrown-up bones;
Eternal dust guides shadowed gangways

To Punic necropolia tombed-out
In timeless tangents, watched by upstart towers
Of a young cathedral, basilicas combed-out
By Time's long competition and the hours

Of each's ruin. The shadows of Jesus
And Hamilcar and the later dead
Back up the ancient argument that whims are diced
Out by the timelessness of heaven. The bled

Lips of this crumbling village, with the cry
Of begging children, prove that stone and scorpion lie.

AUTUMN IN MAJORCA

Autumn again: how many more?
The quiet land broods
In the peace of hope taken away,
Like a birth in silence
Or slipping unnoticed towards Death.

In the dusk and softness of earth's evening
Black figs fall and burst:
Pig food, earth food
Tears from the tree's broad face.

The familiar wind makes passions tolerable:
A woman does not know for whom she sings;
A prophecy of rain when clouds collect
And the earth in its achievement turns
But will not breathe.

ON A TWIN BROTHER'S
RELEASE FROM
A SIBERIAN PRISON CAMP

Out of the snow my brother came
Ghost within ghost like a child's game
Of case into case;
Cloud reflections smashed with wattled feet,
A coniferous stick wielded to meet
Face with face.

Moss-warmed, waist-coated with leaves
His memory survived to shake my hand,
Soil-laden fingers
Reaching from my brother who craves
Impossibly for the enormous land
Where no man lingers.

A surrogate ghost my brother found a road
Across blue ridges, by marks of axe and woad
From Okhotsk shores:
Until frost-bitten both in one grey form
Ghost became brother to an Arctic storm
Beyond all laws.

A price was paid to wilderness and fire:
Flashbacks of his vision beamed
On bleak Siberian snows
Show recollection full of truth and liar:
What one remembers never is what seemed
But what some stranger throws

Up like a ghost before your eyes,
A picture that the ghost of you would see
Had it the power to span
The world from now to then and recognize
What memory discarded and set free
Before you turned and ran.

Each morning my brother asks himself what words
Remain to ply and weave, what dreams, what birds
By twilight to make
Warm nests behind the sockets of his eyes
Opened by gentian-blue barbarian skies
That stayed in his wake.

A youth spent uprooting deciduous nerves
Gave strength to the broad-winding river-curves
Of his soul;
Tenacious eyes sought leaf-mould for breath
Each footstep released what life lived in death
In that great coal-

Forest that froze and murdered yet gave him air
To create a miracle by silent prayer
In my too-undying heart;
My brother became me, memories welded with steel
United in fever and flame, but never to heal,
Only meeting to part.

ON A DEAD BLUEBOTTLE

Dog-fought to its death by folded paper:
An overloaded bluebottle
Crossed the window on a clumsy track
Like a Junkers 52 aimed for Crete.

Survivor of the rains,
With the temerity to try it on
Too long with autumn,
It never knew what happened –

Landed on a matchbox, dead but hardly damaged:
Convenient for what it carried.

One by one its passengers came out:
White-hooded monks debouching
From a still war-painted aircraft
At its dispersal point;
Wriggling over fuselage and wings
As if inspecting flaws after a crash-landing
Of skin and wing that covered
A maggot-cargo from the summer weather,
As if they had paid ticket, food and board
And wanted refund for a trip cut short,
Turned and drew back in lily-whiteness,
Upright with peevish nagging
At some travel agent robber.

Horror was what I felt at filth on filth
Too quickly feeding
To feed the many filthy mouths within,
Horror at the proof of life so powerful
Unsuicidable
Persistent in such ways too small to realize.

For those in need of comfort
That the human race will beat survival
To the end of time
This is it, I thought –

These little bleeders twisting out their time
Are Godsent guarantees
That you and I have season-tickets
For too long to contemplate:
For in the middle of the final maggot
One maggot will survive
To start it all again.

PICTURE OF LOOT

Certain dark underground eyes
Have been set upon
The vast emporiums of London.

Lids blink red
At glittering shops
Houses and museums

Shining at night
Chandeliers of historic establishments
Showing interiors to Tartar eyes.

Certain dark underground eyes
Bearing blood-red sack
The wineskins of centuries

Look hungrily at London:
How many women in London?
A thousand thousand houses

Filled with the world's high living
And fabulous knick-knacks;
Each small glossy machine

By bedside or on table or in bathroom
Is the electrical soul of its owner
The finished heart responding

To needle or gentle current;
And still more houses, endlessly stacked
Asleep with people waiting

To be exploded
The world's maidenhead supine for breaking
By corpuscle Tartars

To whom a toothbrush
Is a miracle;
What vast looting

What jewels of fires
What great cries
And long convoys

Of robbed and robbers
Leaving the sack
Of rich great London.

A CHILD'S DRAWING

A horse in a field drinking water:
A child's drawing (with a tree)
Is how it looks to me
From a bed and through the window.

Village houses stacked behind
But horse made beautiful
Blown into shape
Back bent to water.

My view uncomplicated:
Your eager nostrils drinking
And unseen except by me
Who sees me watching you drinking
Even the slime and water
At the bottom of your pool.

Who – as well as making you –
Put you face to face
(Within the child's drawing of a field
Looking clear into the pool
That children envy)
And me here?

No complaint,
For you have field and tree and water
And I my child's drawing through the window.

OPPOSITES

Fire and water
Chemically meet
In mutual slaughter.

Fire would the other cook:
The evangelical conviction
Of a Six-day Book.

Water would the other kill:
Philanthropy to bring
High temperatures to nil.

Yet ask what solid flesh may stay
Fire with swamp
Water with baked clay;

Neither compound an utter loss:
One left with dregs
And one with dross.

1

How did they begin? What oracular sound
Reached us from platforms underground?
What muzzle moved against the humid clay?
What well-clawed feet scratched into ocular day?

They waited, sleek-bellied rats
Whose memories (kept dry in old tin hats)
Were parchment-read and spread, then lit
As torches to illuminate for these rats
The runnels and the tunnels of each pit.

Revenge was not the fashion: those who shoved
Were put no fatal question, a balanced glove
Ignored upon their shoulders, while in the mines
Unchallenged diggers sent out signs
Of geologic stairways built on bones:
A noise of rodents nosing through the stones.

Where are they now? With perfect guile
They breathe good air and walk such streets above
That glisten with fraternity and love;
In plastic surgery of grim disguise
They sport dark spectacles instead of eyes
Who might be you or me or that false smile
That gives out bread-and-butter in God's name
And silently observes responses – like a game.

Where? No need to look around, my friend
Or in big books that open at the end
(Since legibility is no great tool).
Nowhere. Stand on your head and play the fool.
How? Put out your tongue and shut one eye:
Good. Stay like that until you die.

And then? The rats will still be underground
Snug in their galleries, unsought, unfound
Untried and tied to undermining tricks
Until your houses shiver and collapse like sticks:
They speak corruption, live among its flowers
Proliferate black seeds in April showers.
The heart stops breeding fields of verity
Becomes an eggtimer overworked and spun
By propaganda whose ignoble run
Of words begets not progress but obesity.
One day you'll take your best friend's hand
And feel his fingers turning into sand.

No one will lift the black patch from a warning
Who cannot see the night from too much morning.
So? You ask too many questions, son:
Take off those glasses, and pick up that gun.

2

Those continentals, the funny English say,
Until my brain rebels and with grey
Just logic substitutes for 'English' a word
Many might object to, a label too absurd
To comprehend, a double syllable
That to me will remain unkillable
Like gutter children or an Arab nomad:
Namely I rename an Angle 'OGAD'.

This brain-somersault has made
It suddenly impossible to call
An oak a limetree or a spade a spade
After sixty months meandering
In warm Majorca and coniferous glade
Where many tongues in silent valleys mix
To push my English to the further banks of Styx.

The first grey sago-OGAD met by me
Was on the high grey waves of OGAD sea,
Stamping passports on the ferryboat
Before the mouth of Dover's dismal throat.
Unprivileged aliens in their special queue
Etched their names for white-faced men in blue,
Unbribable stern servants of the realm
Whose rat-like ashen fingers grip the helm
Of OGADLAND, keep an inner circle speed
To guard an obsolescent greed
Of law and order firm behind seven veils
Of self-important mists – and Channel gales.

I lingered in this continental line
Idealizing Britain-of-the Brine
To my American wife with passport green,
Until a tall Sicilian wept and cried
That those grey OGAD cliffs so vaguely seen
Would ever bar his way to Paradise –
Because a leaden-weighted face of ice,
Bilious from its last attack of spleen,
Based his entry on a throw of dice.

Weeping so, he'd do no wrong
I say, but who am I when rubber stamps
And lines of ANGLE-OGAD faces vet
With blank dictatorship these so-called tramps?
Such rats will face the floodtide yet.

3

Many pink-faced OGADS of the north
I have met on Sundays leading forth
Pink-faced OGAD-dogs on lengths of leather
On typical wet days of OGAD weather.

The second month came musically sweet
And mild, blue skies glittering with birdsong
And silver jetplanes frolicking like fleet
Lambs not yet responsible. 'What a
Beautiful raincloud over there!'

Black and grey, yet
Surely a silver-lining lurks somewhere?
How strangely like a mountain, round and jet;
Moving with speed, yet silently, no rain
Falling from its cabbage – no, cauliflower – head:
And suddenly a mushroom grows instead!

Such OGAD weather does not give clear vision
Hides all above the level of the eyes
Makes only power to see with fair precision
Certain orders posted by the wise
Of this dark OGAD world: 'Keep off the grass'
And 'Queue this side of sign'. 'Thou shalt not pass
Unless your child or dog be on a lead'.
'Keep to the left'. 'Slow down'. 'Reduce your speed'.
'Don't park your car upon this hallowed spot'.
'Drop litter here'. (That animals begot?)
'Step along there, room for two inside'.
And not one democrat looked up and sighed:
You need not lift your face towards the sky,
All orders are placed level with the eye.

These pithy messages must make good trade
For those who paint them. A poet's blade
Can't cut more ice, the brains
Of dull bespectacled sad OGAD folk
Are taught by television and a race for trains
Each morning not to test the laden yoke
By a gaze to heaven, when all earthy bread
Is planted firmly at their feet instead.

26

4

Revolution is the word of God
A firefly that lifts from soddened ground
For one second at the end of spring.
So go the workings of the unsound
Mind in its beginnings, a minor sting
That no rat notices, and turns no brown
Last winter's leaf to face the sky.
In this live jungle must the mind leap down
To feed on pickings of dark soil, and shy
Its hawk-beak at the earth's sweet guile:
Then rise full-caloried to kill in style.

These are the commandments of the rats:
You shall be born into the melting-vats
Without an eye to give or a tooth to lose
And never want for schooling, work or shoes.
Good: but each advertisement is a decree
A hanged man on the propaganda tree
(From ITV as well as BBC)
To make it shoot up high and thin:
A hundred thousand may begin
To march one damp October dawn:
You can't thank Life that you were born,
Says Rat beneath his atom-cloud: the melting-vats
Demand obedience to no one but the rats.

You shall love the rats who take the hours
From your clumsy hands, who guide you over roads
And traffic islands, take heavy loads
From lighter brains, give paper flowers
Of happiness, and stand you in a line
For bus or train, transport you to a house
And television set and OGAD wine:
You too can be a rat divine
A living civil servant of a louse
Though first you must become a mouse.

O hear me, soulless OGADS of the mist
Older than the rocks on which you pissed
The winter snows away for idle summer;
Listen to the rawboned pitprop drummer
Who versifies rebellion from the ice
(In exile where he feeds on uncooked rice
That one day will explode his walnut fist)
Hear his warning over your contented mummer
And the mewings of devoted mice:
Catastrophe will be the last device.

5

So keep your whiskers weaving while you may
Beneath blue helmets, antennae of the law
Sensitively finding those who pray
For criminal success by some shop door.
The time to strike is now. Drop your club
Upon the head that holds ideas to boast
Your kill, who stands like an untamed cub
For buses on the wrong side of the post.

Keep your long rat-whiskers sleek
The man with garden shears may die next week
Next month, yet maybe come with fist and claw
With fuses primed in a Beethoven score
And dynamite ensconced in crated butter.
You do not even hear them mutter.
They watch you pace (from behind a shutter)
See you preen your whiskers as you walk
Twirl your truncheon, chew your rind of pork
Watch a drunk negotiate the street
(Correctly). You glance at the callbox of your power
Blind to their refusal of defeat
As they debate on when to name the hour.

King Rodent reigns on OGAD demock-rats
On water rats that watch each riverbank
And bridge for criminals who do not thank
King Rodent's riddance of white leopard cats:
They wait until the shadow's leap
Becomes an offer of a well-aired bed
That does not promise them a life of sleep.

King Happiness has waved his magic wand
Shown you a smooth reflection in the pond
Of television shows, recorded your own voice
In the self-selections of your choice,
Set up his directions on the street
Turned mechanic to your motorbikes
Poured patriot sauce upon your luncheon meat
Sent you out on Sunday-morning hikes:
Party-hatted happiness is here,
Each tenet brayed by a Royal Chanticleer.

6

Death is not preferable (had you
Considered it?) to this untrue-
To-life and that man's sweated brow.
How could an end called Death
End this as easily as that
Man thinks? Questions come
From artesian springs
Labyrinths of sea and soil
Making question marks
Out of eternal water
Demanding bloody answers
And a bloody year
Of cleansing. Slaughter?

Here comes the First Battalion
Television Light Infantry
With bayonets fixed –
Break them down!

Around the left flank come
The Porno Paper Cavalry Corps
Riding pink and yellow tanks –
Cut them off!

Under your feet spring
The Rat-State Sapper Brigade:
Dig them over like a garden
Do not let their forces overwhelm you
Rather go insane before they
Force you to their ranks
Or kill you.

The pyrotechnic paranoia of the anti-rats:
Clean against dark
Light opposing Death
Tearing slide-rule and scalpel, pen and typewriter,
Scales of rat-justice, rat-precision,
Libraries recording rat-right and rat-wrong
Rats that nip away each toe
And suck the soles of too thin feet
Rats that eat your eyes like oysters
Spread false trails over burrowed hills
Swamp-rats wood-rats tree rats
Plague-rats, pet-rats, army and police-rats
Sadistic rats that will not kill
Kind rats that drug you in the night
Rats that let you crush them in the garden
Run across your path
Climb trees before you see them
Eat corn that would give you the strength to kill them

Rats that laugh, rats that fill the night with infants crying
Rats that gloat, rats that bend your life before them
Rats that move around you in the night
Rats invisible that ring you during day
Rats in books, on radios, in tins of food
On television screens, rats behind
A million miles of counters
Wielding guide-books, tables, catalogues
Slide-rules, stethoscopes, maps
Election registers, passports, insurance stamps
Death certificates, prison records
Visas, references, forms to sign
Case histories, birth certificates
Statistics, interview reports
Personality tests, loyalty rating
And knives to cure
The pyrotechnic paranoia of the anti-rats.

7

The city is seething with discontent
For they all wonder where the deserters went:
They took no beer and they took no bread
And everyone says that they must be dead:
Some speak with anger (a few speak with tears)
But most out of vague speculatory fears
That they still live among us, active and thin
Or are out in the wilderness about to dig in
And return to besiege us when winter has fled.

The deserters are waiting without beer or bread
Around ancient fires of obstinate coke,
And they laugh in the city and wonder who spoke
When the wind lifts a flame from wilderness fires
(Caught in snowlight – quickly expires)
They look up and listen from parlour debates
Then resume their relinquished sensory states
Within and without their crumbling walls,
Like jungle tigers secure in their night
When the forlorn bark of the jackal calls.

8

Behind the rat-horizons of the world
Try to decipher what history has hurled
Against the white range of your exposed spine;
Sit in your isolated jungle and define
(Among pine-needles and a flask of wine)
Your lack of Revolutionary fire
Love of safety (number one desire)
Happily tied to the waterwheel
For irrigation that will soon congeal
Blood in brain and arms, will sit you still
And quiet while the busy rats distil
Sweet liquor as a chaser for each pill
That saps away the flame of heart and will.

You found it hard to struggle for house and bread
To hone a sword and guide a plough
Found the ache too much for your tread
From one loaf to another, held your head
Low because you killed the man who stood
Before you for a faggot of dry wood.

Sailing from one coast to another grew
Wearying. You wanted women and a mild brew
To dull what wits the day's work left sound,
To sleep your life out on dry ground
Find a warm hut and a midnight glow,
A woman clothed in black from head to toe.

Sling, spear, plough, lathe and pen
Made artificers of house and den
Weighed power on scales and gave books of law
To save you from the blight of fang and claw,
Until this comfort to Utopia goes
Beyond a golden mean and throws

Us into progress where perfection flags:
Scarecrows beneath banners of atomic rags.

Like Zeno's arrow the motion is but sure:
From good to bad or bad to good:
No ship stood in stillness pure
Moved north or south in flood-
Tide and wild wind, or smartly drove
Its mainsail back to struggle and song
After a doldrum residence wherein wove
Sea-dolphins – opium to the eyes in long
Performance. Either move,
Or the sea swells into another form,
Little choice between calm and storm.

Each man wants to move the boat
Clockwise with fashionable hands
Reading history on how to float
Upon the wash with watermusic bands.
One calls the tune but others play the music
And idle waves of Neptune make the crew sick.

The rats devise solutions for each lake
Each overture and song reduce to easy,
Fix stabilizers firm from wind to wake:
And still the crew persist in feeling queasy.

Old antagonisms rage:
Rat-machinations roped with force
Imprison beauty in a cage,
Encircle it with propaganda morse.

'Corruption is corruption, sometimes sweet
Is only dangerous when it stagnates:
Corrupt before, corrupted ever
Only keep it moving to be safe.'

35

First Rat: Feed, house, educate and teach
Place anti-seasick tablets in their reach.
Second Rat: Dope, rope, spiflicate and preach
Colour them by sunray lamps or bleach.

Third Rat: Dazzle, flash, warp their speech
Send them every Sunday to the beach.
Fourth Rat: Deceive, demand, even beseech
Cleverly, cleverly – they'll never screech!

9

Retreat like Scythians, like men of hair
Back into folding earth and lair:
Burn and scorch black the rich fields that you leave,
Once tilled with freedom and passion-verse.

Prepare to destroy that for which you grieve:
It is already ruined by the worse
Rat venom. Do not wish for what was there
Before Rats came but keep the cleansed air
Uncloyed, devoid of devil-noses
And perverted paper roses
Who pander to each scheme that rat proposes.

When on the rack-and-pinion of retreat
Earn your wayside cigarettes and bread
By giving lessons on the rats' defeat
Disguised in languages more live than dead:
Tutor yourselves in map-reading and crime
And devil's courage for the bleak time

When you alone will face the empty plain
Armed only with a visionary brain
That tried to understand how earth and sky
Could meet beyond the reach of feet and eye.

The would-be Rat-destroyers may feel this:
Burdened with a glimpse of emptiness
Night after night, with dreams that kiss
Despair as a king's seal, and nothingness:
A dull light gleaming on continual fight
In a retreat that leads beyond the end of night.

10

It was a rabbit skin, without meat
That took me to the fleapit for a treat:
The wasteland that seemed to Mr Eliot death
Nurtured me with passion, life and breath
To prolong for one more generation
A wasteland satellite of veneration:
A bottle-top, a piece of bone, a stone
Marked on no posters or big banners
To catapult against the rodent planners.

. . . the rock stop and turbo-drill that goes
Through granite like a knife through butter
(Shall I follow Mr Eliot's nose
And clinch this verse by using 'gutter'?)
Rock-a-bye-baby, reach the tree top
Sing as you reap the apple crop;
Rob each garbled voice of Wednesday's ash
Ring out the mardi gras to grab and smash:
Hook-up your ribbons to a new Maypole.

The wasteland was a place where I best played
As a snotty-nosed bottle-chasing raggèd-arsed kid:
From a rusty frame and two cot-wheels I made
A bike that took me on a roll and skid
Between canal banks, tip and plain
And junk shops advertising 'Guns for Spain'.

I read the tadpole angler quite complete
What Katy did at her first Christmas treat
Envied Monte Cristo's endless riches
But not Eliza's shame at her dropped stitches,
The splendid sack of Usher's houses
By philanthropists with ragged trousers.
In wintertime were rabbit skins fair game
For keeping warm the embers of such knowledge:
The wasteland was my library and college.

11

What's past is past, what still to come:
King, queen and godhead of Time's guide.
Show your bottom-dogs and sparkling fangs
In conspiratorial well-clawed gangs.
Open Baedeker's *Handbook to the Jungle*
A thin-leaved blood-bound untried book to plan
All expeditions on, and scan
Its well-mapped footpaths (thornbush to the right):
Mined offices avoid at any cost;
Advice from all contributors is sound
Gathered by ears pressed firmly to the ground.

Ignore policemen if you're lost
By-pass the Customs, frontier weak at X
Step on the skeletons of vanguard wrecks
Hillslopes good for cover, summit wrong,
Travellers had better go by night
And eat ripe berries as they walk along.

Landmarks described with economic prose:
This cathedral has a mildewed nose
From decades of unmedicated sores.
Decay comes quicker when it flouts Time's laws.

See this castle? Rotten doors:
King left owing bills for bread and cheese
Queen stored perfumes in deepfreeze
Was tricked for absolution with the whores.

Take those statues by the wall
Carved on a diet of olive-oil and gall:
Unbribable stern servants of the realm
Turned up their noses and let go the helm.

12

Watch the sky. Watch the warning
Floating down of an autumn morning.
Barricade your colleges and schools
Sharpen slide-rules into fighting tools.
Paper to a depth of thirty inches
May stop a bullet and prove good defences,
But fire will desolate consume and scorch
That to begin needs but a single torch.
A red sky at night will be their delight
And red in the morning the Rats' night dawning.

Admitted, you gave them ale and telly
But in return took each man's name and age
And locked his magic in a wicker cage
Burning it in secret while they filled
Unwittingly their bellies after hunger.

You cannot read the writing on the wall:
They were not given bread at all
But food to make them strong (and sane)
Enough to understand your orders.

A meal of pure white bread is bad
When given to a dog the dog goes mad.
The bread of life is of a different grain
It feeds the body wholemeal and the brain.

13

Slowly, slowly, Dungeness lighthouse
Dim in the distance dipped its wick:
Old Folkestone vowed to thee its country
And Beachy Head was being sick;

But stouter England stood and stouter
From Berwick's Tweed to Dover Castle
Hugging the Downs beneath its arm
Like an empty paper parcel;

And slowly also big Cape Grey Nose
Lays itself before the boat
Sends its white birds up to catch my
Soul while yet it stays afloat.

14

Retreat, dig in, retreat
Withdraw your shadow from the crimson
Gutters that run riot down the street.

Retreat, dig in, arrange your coat
As a protective covering
A clever camouflage of antidote.

Retreat still more, still more
Remembering your images and words:
Perfect the principles of fang-and-claw.

The shadows of retreat are wide
Town and desert equally bereft
Of honest hieroglyph or guide.

Release your territory and retreat
Record preserve and memorize
The journey where no drums can rouse nor beat:

Defeat is not the question. Withdraw
Into the hollows of the hills
Until this winter passes into thaw.

Dig in no more. Turn round and fight
Forget the wicked and regret the lame
And travel back the way you came,
In front the darkness, and behind – THE LIGHT.

from A Falling Out of Love
and Other Poems, 1964

POEM LEFT BY
A DEAD MAN

Let no one say I was cleaning this gun:
I killed myself because
I wanted the sun
But got the moon.
Sanity came back too soon.

I did not even clean the gun:
Put in two bullets for the moon and sun
Spun the chamber in a final game.
The sun and moon were both the same.

Borrow got here, so did I
Nothing in front but sea and sky.
Blue, traditional, unplanned,
Then white with envy at safe land:
Were such cold acres ever seen
Than vast and climbing for this rock?

Big as the fish that got away,
Bigger, but no one ever died from shock
At so much water, such wide space:
Vostok III and Vostok IV
Slap proportion in the face.

Rapier-thin horizons claw
At blasé tissue of bland eye:
While Man is climbing at the moon
The sea foams white on every shore,
Moonstruck where the start began
Moonlit in the wake of Man
Who turns his back on Finisterre.

WOODS

Woods are for observing from a distance
On your father's arms:
Woods are for being frightened of –
Bogie-men swing among those close-packed trees.

Woods are then for making fires in
Running before the wrath of cop or farmer:
Smoke and the smell of dandelions
In place of blood.

Later for loving girls in:
Untidy bushes lick damp hair,
Secret, dark and out of sight
With nothing now to replace blood.

Some use woods for attacking and defending
The black scream of unnatural possession,
Tree roots linchpinned into earth
By shudders and the soil of death.

By summer shunned in fear of lightning
The bitter roaming flash of snaked lightning;
In winter shelter us from rain or snow:
Tree-packs hold our fate like cards.

Woods are then forgotten two-score years
Power lapsing into midnight dreams,
The core of body and soul
Scooped by the knife of living.

The wood became jungle, and you its shadow:
Woods a purple rage of wakened dogs,
To be kept out of, snubbed
Hemmed into night, not known.

Woods returned, tamed, not for
Making love or fires in.
Familiar; suspicious of their shelter
You stay at home in rain or snow –

The woods are seen but not remembered
A far-off shadow, cloud or dream;
Your power vanishes with their's –
No more to be defended, or attacked.

STORM

Safe from horizontal rain
And gale-blown boxing-gloves thumping the walls
The wireless plays a drama
Of a poet stricken at a priest's house
Reached only by footpath,
A poet descending Jacob's ladder made of sand
Washed by mountain torrents,
Spouting rhetoric of fire as he fell –

While kilocycles off frequency
Morse code mewed by strophe and antistrophe
Behind the stark undoing of the poet
Lost in narrow seams of God and Sin and Death,
Corroded by the opposite of what he would be.

The code comes in again, a querulous demand
Plucked by a far-off guitar with one string left
That chance may hear,
And through the poet's white despair
The rhythmic images cry distraction,
Till I read their symbols
That beyond my bosom-comfort
A ship by chance of time committed
To elemental wrath in asking for anchorage
From blind and twisting waves:
Five score sailors on the sea
Never to be compared to a suffering poet in his anguish.

HOUSEWIFE

A housewife sweeps her doorstep
Pavement yard and walls
Each leaf of wilting privet
Polishes the window
To do away with dust and bloodmarks
In case one speck shows sin.

Kills all trace by art and elbow as if dirt
Smears the dark side of her mirror face –
As proof of jungle ape and missing link
That drags back to when we hopped
From the saltpan slime of Lake Bacteria,
That first jelly-blob deviously edging
Towards moondust and the feat of sleep,
Sunstroke, blight of spoiled nerves,
Weapons and a new flint-hack for food –
And then the bright machinegun.

She sweeps to lovingly dispose
Of bigstar jellyfish and show-off crabs
That wriggle before the new damp
Jungle world of hoofprints, spoor
Half-chewed herbivore and worse –
Beaten after twilight years by her stout arms,
And an evolutionary smile.

STARS

Stars, seen through midnight windows
Of earth-grained eyes
Are fullstops ending invisible sentences,
Aphorisms, quips, mottoes of the gods
Indicate what might have been made clear
Had words stayed plain before them.

Criss-crossed endlessly for those who read,
Each light-year sentence testifies how far
Life spreads, and how those full stops
Go on living after necks cease aching.

In observing them, the bones relax:
Eyes close when we are dead
And they have stared all poets out.
Full stops are beautiful as stars,

Each glowing with the light of people vanished
From the continually red-burned earth
Fuelled by those whose outward eye drinks fever
And inward eye harnesses their shadows

To read what never had been written
Until, drunk with Charioteers, Animals and Goddesses,
Conjurers, Club-men, Fish and Magic Boxes
Full stops are joined with words shaped into poems
Ending with full stops as meaningful as stars.

Yes – definitively to some wrongful deed
And ending like a quick knife to a knot,
Is a serpent-lover singing to be freed
From no and negative and nothing gained.

Hard to fix decisions as to yea and nay
While needing the when and how: near-questions
Aimed to draw that final sibilant and vow
To upright-positive and all to win.

Success for lovers and conspirators
Unlocks the sins that grace a thousand lips;
Dogs bark, and babies cry at meeting air:
(Whether yes or no is hardly to be known)

But if affirmative, are guessings at the guess
That darkness is nothing but a final yes.

DEAD MAN'S GRAVE

Three sons in silence by their father's grave
Think of the live man
Not yet split in three by blackness –
Cannot cross the limbo zone,
Reach him who went a year ago through.

Mute before grass bending:
Headstones grey and white proliferate,
Stumps in a shell-shocked forest
Making question and exclamation mark;
They talk about flowers from a visit
When water in the vase was ice
On this plateau exposed to collieries
And winds bailing out Death's
Deepest coffers it was so cold;
Of how frost to prove the dead not dead
Turned the water iron-white,
Swollen muscle garrotting the flowers
Till the vase exploded,
By trying its own strength out on itself –
Scattered petals to a dozen graves.

Three brothers stand in silence,
Feel the strength the father lost.

THE DROWNED
SHROPSHIRE WOMAN

Narrow in the back
She played all day with fishes
Watched them go like arrows
Through aerated water
Between her legs and dodge
The fantail spread of fingers.

She was crossed in love:
Water hurtling loinwards and into heart
Found another hiding-place and pool
Where sharper arrows
Played upon her sorrow,
And sunlight on her stooping
Made more voracious fishes breed.

She was narrow in the back
And played all night at fishes,
Wading for the biggest of them all
By moon and guile
Out from the reedy bank,
Until by unlit dawn
A fisherman in silence
Drew his silent catchnet down.

Green fishes fled through lightgreen water
Flint heads with moulded eyes
Chipping at infiltrating light,
And switching to the
White legs of the Shropshire woman,
Played tag in the blue beams
Of her impenetrable eyes,
Between the whitening flesh
Of open fingers.

CAR FIGHTS CAT

In a London crescent curving vast
A cat sat –
Between two rows of molar houses,
Birdsky in each grinning gap.

Cat small – coal and snow
Road wide – a zone of tar set hard and fast:
Four-wheeled speedboats cutting a dash
For it
From time to time.

King Cat stalked warily midstream
As if silence were no warning on this empty road
Where even a man would certainly have crossed
With hands in pockets and been whistling.

Cat heard, but royalty and indolence
Weighed its paws to hobnailed boots
Held it from the dragon's-teeth of safety first and last,
Until a Daimler scurrying from work
Caused cat to stop and wonder where it came from –
Instead of zig-zag scattering to hide itself.

Maybe a deaf malevolence descended
And cat thought car would pass in front,
So spun and walked all fur and confidence
Into the dreadful tyre-treads . . .
A wheel caught hold of it and
FEARSOME THUDS
Sounded from the night-time of black axles in
UNEQUAL FIGHT
That stopped the heart to hear it.

But cat shot out with limbs still solid,
Bolted, spitting fire and gravel
At unjust God who built such massive
Catproof motorcars in his graven image,
Its mind made up to lose and therefore learn,
By winging towards
The wisdom toothgaps of the canyon houses
LEGS AND BRAIN INTACT.

FROG IN TANGIER

A frog jumped
Feebly along the pool edge
Away from the trapnet of my feet.
I picked it up.
A pink wound shone
Between belly and that phosphorous
Faint zig-zag down its back,
Pain the colour of pomegranate
And orange agony,
Umbilical string hanging
A catchline towards water
Yet dragging like an anchor
That weighed the entire world
When it tried to jump.

Had it been pierced by a snake?
Clipped by a wind-thrown tree
Cut by scorpion, bird or pruning hook?
Or was it a festering frog-cancer
That gathered and burst after a life
Of statue-cunning,
Too much patience before
Each silent nerve-leap
Onto a dreamy insect?

I hoped the magic water
Would seal its wound
Stitch back outflowing life.
It swam deep under,
Air bubbles snapping
Like fleas abandoning a mouse,
Messages from its stopped body
Breaking at trees and sky.

It was a leaf suspended
Four legs and green spade-head,
Flayed rushblades clear
Above the indeterminate green
Basin of the pool;
Calmed between earth and air
Dying in its native water
From my allowing a leap
Into the safety of its death
When it wanted peace
And a long quiet end
Lasting a lifetime.

It hung in the float-still water,
Next day gone:
Mud-guns exploded
By assaulting minnow-snouts.
From nightcaves underwater
Daylight filters like a ghost
To scare marauding goldfish
Chewing mosquito eggs –
And to illuminate
A hundred minnows savaging my spit.

FRIEND DIED

Tears stop, and suffering
Goes the next level down,
Deeper when tears won't start.
Pain outlives, the hollow soul burns
Till cured by nothing less
Than the same death for me.

You are world-finished
Blacked out, sea-driven
Beyond soil and nowhere,
Empty caves filled
By your heavy death-weighing:

The sea and moon fought
And their vicious clamour killed
The survivor who is empty
And the winner who is dead.

GUIDE TO
THE TIFLIS RAILWAY

The witnessed scenery changes
To sunbaked cliffs and spun dry trees:
Parched and monotonous hill country.

No one has the will to stop the train,
Though all can now observe what's to be seen:
A priest embalming a dissected brain.

Hardly visible from the railway
A deep ravine throws out its endless bile.
We cross the river, and notice to the left
Various vertical caves in Gothic style

Which afforded refuge to the Christians,
Sparse and lean (a rouble to the guide)
Against the Mongols and the Persians
Who swam the Caspian like cats against no tide;

Who one time sent three gifts from Samarkand
Of frugal sunlight to an ancient feast:
Now reaping a reward with scarlet swords
From the full belly of the fecund East.

Our train proceeds, unfolds an arrowmark of bones,
The valley widens, easy to foretell
That crossing the military road we soon
Reach the city and look up the best hotel.

from Love in the Environs of Voronezh and Other Poems *and* Storm and Other Poems, 1968 and 1974

BABY

A small man formed
One hour after forging into light,
Body-brain wrapped and blue eyes
Open to noise of rook and cuckoo
To stalk a rabbit in the meadow
Read a book, nothing less than
Blank before sudden turns
To evergreen or glint of water.

Hirsute and stern on bleak arrival
He lay down after a toiler's day
Face to say: All right.
You gave me life, but death also.

Forehead creased on future worry
When hacking obstacles,
Indenting map-hair on moving palm
To say it doesn't matter, go to sleep.
Struck a lifeline horoscope
Of luck, speedkid, handy with women –
Which years will balance
In give, take or ruination,
Seeing all but never everything.

Sleep beyond the iced bite of the moon,
Being what you are this moment
Free with innocence but lacking milk
Soon to become all you do not feel,
Advancing against
The normal hazarding inroads
That spin life into havoc:
Power to dissect visions
Like the yolk and mucus of an egg,
And build up certain freedoms from the moon.

TREE

A broad and solid oak exploded
Split by mystery and shock
Broken like bread
Like a flower shaken.
Acorn guts dropped out:
A dead gorilla unlocked from breeding trees,
Acorns with death in their baby eyes.

A hang-armed scarecrow in the wind:
What hit it? Got into it? Struck
So quietly between dawn and daylight?
With a dying grin and wooden wink
A lost interior cell relinquished its ghost:
In full spleen and abundant acorn
A horn of lightning gored it to the quick.

Trees move on Fenland
Uprooting men and houses on a march
To reach their enemy the sea.
Silent at the smell of watersalt
Treelines advance. The sea lies low,
Snake-noise riding on unruffled surf
While all trees wither and retreat.

Out of farm range or cottage eyes trees make war
Green heads close as if to kiss
Roots to rip at quickening wood of tree-hearts
And tree-lungs, sap-running wood-flesh
Hurled at the moon, breaking oak
Like the dismemberment of ships,
At the truce of dawn wind trumpeting.

Sedate, dispassionate and beautiful
They know about panic and life and patience
Grow by guile into night's
Companions and day's evil
Setting landmarks and boundaries
That fight the worms.

Trees love, love love, love Death
Love a windscorched earth and copper sky
Love the burns of ice and fire
When lightning as a last hope is called in.
Boats on land they loathe the sea
And wait with all arms spread to catch the moon:
Pull back my skin and there is bark
Peel off my bark and there is skin:
I am a tree whose roots destroy me.

DITCHLING BEACON

End of life and before death
Feathers dipping towards oaken frost
A bird heard that shot:
The ink sky burst,
Stone colliding with the sun

Echo stunned its wing
String hauled it down.
Gamekeeper or poacher
Cut its free flight to the sea.

Vice had tongue, veins, teeth
Dogs in panoply, pressure
To ring a sunspot fitting neat
The blacked-out circle of a gun.

LIZARD

Fiddle-tongue and spite
Hang as if asleep
Safe on his tipped world,
But lizard-shoulders hunch
Pulsate at a fly on slanting wall.

Belly smooth, feet stuck firm
A thousand volts of paralyzing tongue
Rifle out and kill;
Weapons in one stomach pit.

Death is quick when looked on,
Sweet as food when the lamps of paradise
Blacken a brain that one day
Hoped to know.

Sparking tongue ignites
A common wink and into oblivion:
The lizard unaware of upside down
Eats as it runs.

EMPTY QUARTER

He meditates on the Empty Quarter:
Mosque of sand dissolving through eggtimer's
Neck. Looks on camel-loads
Starting for Oman or Muscat
By invisible Mercator's thread
That burns the hoof and shrivels
All humps of water. Empty Quarter lures,
He travels with his heaped caravan
Earth-tracks marked as lines
Of unstable land, golden sandgrit
Lifting up grey dunes near vulcan-
Trees and foul magnesium wells
That asps and camels drink from.
He throws off bells, beads, silk, guns
Knives and slippers, scattering all
No longer needed – camel meat
For scavengers, everything
But his own dishrags of flesh.

Naked and demented he hugs
A tree rooted in the widest waste
Catching dew from God at dawn
And dates dropping through rottenness,
Tastes the lone tree's shade
No one can chop or whip him from,
Till one day ravelled in his own white flame
He abandons the Empty Quarter
And trudges back to terrify the world.

FIRST POEM

Burned out, burned out
Water of rivers hold me
On a course towards the sea.
Burned out was like a tree
Cut down and hollowed
No branches left
Seasoned by fire into a boat:
Burned out through love's
Wilful spending
Yet sure it will float
Kindle a fresh blaze
Burn out again
On a stranger shore –
Unless pyromaniac emotions
Scorch me in midstream
And the sun turns black.

LOVE'S MANSION

To keep them healthily in thrall
They build a little fire in the hall –
And burn their opulent home to ash.
A ruin is better than no love at all.

Dark and ageing timbers crash
Cats surround it at full moon.
Did they abandon love too soon
Full of happiness to see it fall?

Let it fall, in sight of all
It kept them long enough in thrall
As cupboards burn and timbers fall.

They're still inside, nowhere to run
No windows through which they can crawl;
Only the trapped and burning see it fall.

It kept them like a snake in thrall.
A ruin is better than no love at all.
They smile unhappily to see it fall.

TO BURN OUT LOVE

To burn out love is to burn a star from the sky
But can touch reach so far,
Feel the fire increase
Careful the heart but not the star will burn?

Star that pulsates like a fish:
My heart meets you in dark or light
To taste the waters of the star which says:
Trust once gone can never be restored –
Such love can surely be put out,
The power to break its fire with my fist.

SEATALK

Talking on the beach:
Love has broken its heart
Is a pomegranate split
A waterfall pouring in.
Each half lifts
Drifts out to sea,
Eaten clean as January boats
By frost and salt.

One will sink, one go free:
Withered fruit-husk without salt
Or soul. Could be you
And could be me, watching January waves
Erupt like whales and thrones and tractors:
Stones clash back into their places.

You wait for a boat to come
And snatch you from love's pandemonium
Of humping tide and screeching stones.
But what shipwrecked you there?
Want to know, and cease to wonder:
The boat lurches into seas of danger
Waves turning phosphorous, turn fire:
Rowers begin work, and you not with them
When the numbness in you burns
Because you do not want to go, or stay.

Pomegranate is a far-off fruit
Scattered seeds fulfil no circle.
Love cannot kill
A broken heart, nor mend it.
The sea defends its dead
And those born from it,
Believes in broken hearts
Burns when it boils so.
No boat can stay, must fall apart
Floating through the open heart,
Like fruit bursting
At the shock of moonless water,
And two more hearts pulled in to slaughter.

NAKED

Naked, naked, I never see you naked
As if to be naked is to tell lies
With the body that you show –
Cover it and keep the truth.

Hide naked, keep it close
You never let me see you naked
Unless half so by accident or tease.
Hide it carefully: those lies are yours,

Not mine, speak them loudly if they burn.
Belong to someone else, not mine.
I see you naked through them,
Through love, naked beyond the truth

That will not let you see yourself.
Keep your body for someone else:
The lies that hide you are less sure
Than the truth that blinds me.

GHOSTS: WHAT JASON SAID TO MEDEA

It is time to part, before murder is done.
We have robbed each other of all we had,
Eaten bitter herbs of battleground and kitchen
And soaked our souls in them,
Digested the gall of trust so cannot give it back
In that pure state it was before:
Consumed ourselves by ignoble hatred.
So let us part like ghosts
And promise not to haunt each other –
Or make ghosts of others.

HUNGER

I haven't found my hunger yet. When will I know
The hunger to eat these walls away?
The smallest creature visible to the eye
Ran the pallid whiteness up this page
And when I crushed it, hungry at its freedom,
I found a tiny spider made of brick.
It had lived on brick, the bright red dust of brick
That filled its dust-dot of a body and even the speck
Of legs it ran upon. Its life was fed by dust,
The dust of bricks, and it had slaked its hunger
On bricks, no question asked or thought of,
Eating through walls was its life, its vital hunger
For the walls it ate through, even at times
Without hunger. It was so realized
I crushed it, a reddish smear
On the page to remind me
Of the hunger that I know about at last.

HEPHZIBAH

Why don't I write or speak the name?
No light at Hephzibah's window,
So do not use 'love' in vain
Nor easily at this turn of the game.
Her name ignites the wind, breeds
Smoke in the snow of the heart
Gluttons the marrow as I watch
The bombed space
Phosphorized to blindness.
You cannot answer letters or my speeches,
A different man when salt burns
Till there is no more light.
Signals change before the gale
Wipes all traffic out.
Cogs and linchpins tattoo Hephzibah
So I can't forget your name, or use it,
But continually hear magic syllables
Shriller than my curse
As I speed through
White headlights flooding the world.

FULL MOON'S TONGUE

She said, when the full moon's tongue hung
Over Earls Court chimneypots,
And he circled slowly
Round the square to find
A suitable parking place –
She said: 'Let's go away together.'

'Keep clear,' he said. 'You'd better not.
I'll take you, but watch out,
For I will bring you back
If at all,
In two pieces.'

She said: 'I'll never want to come back
If I go away with you.'

'They all do,' he said.
'I'll bring you back in two pieces
And you'll live like that forever
And never join them up again.'
'How cruel,' she said, seeing what he meant.

'Oh no,' he said. 'To take you apart completely
From yourself and make two separate pieces
Might be the one sure way of fixing
A whole person out of you –
Some do, some don't.'
He was exceptionally nonchalant.

'I'm not sure now,' she said,
Screaming suddenly: 'You bastard!
Let me get out, I want to walk.'

He stopped the car
But could not park it,
Someone with a similar problem
Was hooting him to move,
So she jumped free and walked away
Leaving him bewildered,
And in at least two pieces.

You talk too much,
Said one piece to another.

Silence and stillness
Are most prized in a whirlwind.
Panic is being caught
Between millstones of stillness –
Feel the bones of the body
Living out the heart's pain.

The whirlwind will penetrate
The stockade of a gaze erected
That nothing can break through,
While waiting for the force
That will pull you into the body
And draw all pain away.

A lawn grows in the palm of one hand:
Trees in the other combust
To chase worms out.
Nothing can soothe the battered soul,
But love cauterizes madness.

SMILE

Can't get him out –
Sits right in the fireplace
Curled up tight
Olive logs send red flames
Feeling the chimney spout.

Cold and safe, legs indrawn,
Wan smile, squats in his fireplace,
Irons cold, hair neat
Away and safe unless
A crowbar can prise him whimpering free.
He smiles wanly because no one has.

If and when he would be normal,
A dead man on the street, smiles
In a mirror no one can smash:
A moonless grimace of victory,
Insane as the sun
That cleanses better than any fire
Or his prison it once burned in.

CHAIN

The chain is weakest at its strongest point:
The strong link by its heart helps weaker parts,
And so weak links grow tauter than they should.

Thus, taking too much strength
The whole chain crumbles
Broken at both weak and stronger points.

Water breaks the strongest chain
When a stormtide drags the ship away.
Power changes all equations –

The strongest link a strand of hair,
And weakest at its strongest point
Shares its heart with weaker hearts.

GULF OF BOTHNIA –
ON THE WAY TO RUSSIA

Midnight aches at the length of life
The endless day
Blocking the porthole-elbow of Bothnia:
One grand eye lit in twelve o'clock yellow,
Turquoise and carmine sun
A wound gouged by the night-dragon
Not yet asleep.

Day bleeds to death
Sea close enough to dip
The pen and write in.
No midsummer howitzer can give
A morphine blast and send the sun
To whatever will rise up at dawn for me.

Space and midnight fill all emptiness,
As lost love bleeds acidic dreams
Into the solvent sea:
Red like a Roman bath.

EURASIAN JETNOTE

Frontiers meet over steppe and meadow
At burial mound, salt waste or winter hut,
Beyond danubes and caspians
Where sturgeon breed by reed and barge-hull –

But wood outlives
Asia or Europe, love shaped by heart-torn
Internal bleeding of the stricken forest.
Wood dies, and is born again.

IRKUTSK

In Irkutsk a swastika was scrawled
On a wall so I took my handkerchief
And spat and rubbed
But it was tough chalk
Wondering why those Red pedestrians
Didn't grind it off.

I'd done the same in London
Walking to the Tube
And missing the train quite often,
But here it was ineradicable Russian chalk
Though I chafed it to the barest shadow,
No one taking notice on their walk
Down Karl Marx Street. I strolled
Away to let them keep it.

Apart from scraping out a concave mark
The crippled cross would stay forever,
And anyway why should I get arrested
For damaging The People's Property?

BAIKAL LAKE-DUSK

Black ice breaking without sound or reason:
Water below moves its shoulders
Like a giant craving to see snow.

Ninety-degree cold preserves mosquito eggs
As the fist of winter
Pulls into the sun's mittens.

The domed sun touches the horizon,
A totem in the lake sinking
Till its feet touch bottom and reach fire.

SHAMAN
AT LISTVYANKA

Stopped his cart
Refused food
Shook tin brass skulls copper
Turned to the sun
And pressed a horseshoe to his eyes
Spun a waterspout of words
Grave toes patterning the soil
Under a tree clothed all in green,
Chews beansprouts from his crown
Spins to pipe dance
Head between land and sky
Hand five candle-fingers
Fuelled by the gutters of his stomach.

Spins to music
Stick legs strut
In wide skin trousers:
Shouting melts and planctifies
Fisherboats and floating logs:
Recites alone and long
On Baikal fish and stork in one:
Sea that threatens fire-spiders
Copperbacks and claws –
Creep from the rimline lake
Feet to feel and lips to taste,
Have no heart but swarm
To eat from him and die of it –
As brass-hooved breakers
Break and draw them back
And he weaving

Over sand to green land
Melting and metalling
In blacksmith power.
Horses birds and torches flee
From tundra magic keening,
Flesh of man flying
Skinflags unfurling
In a merciless slipstream to the sun.

Drop, hear drums
Rend on the flight,
He so far within
Sly, taciturn and a bully when normal
Knowing he must keep that self out
Or power goes,
Be an old man forever
Carved in rock by the fire
After the last telling.

TOASTING

Drink, blackout, gutter-bout
Kick back nine swills of vodka
That put an iron band around
Thorned skullcap and fire
Of words toasting Life
Peace, Town or Cousin.

Bottles, heaped grub, dead towers in tabletown:
Wine descends in light and colour
As if the Devil had a straw stuck there
Greedily drawing liquid in
As consciousness draws out.

RAILWAY STATION

Death is the apotheosis of the Bourgeois Ethic.
Tolstoy when he felt it coming on
Left his family and set out for Jerusalem.

Death shared its railway station:
He in a coma heard trains banging
Where Anna violated life.

The fourth bell drowned his final wrath.
The Bolsheviks renamed the station after him
Instead of Bourgeois Death.

RIDE IT OUT

Ride it out, ride it,
Ride out this mare of sleeplessness
Galloping above the traffic roar
Of Gorki Street,
Weaving between Red stars
And the grind of cleaning wagons.
Today all Moscow was in mourning
Because there's no queue at Lenin's tomb.
I told them but they wouldn't believe me.

Ride out this beast who won't let me sleep,
Drags me up great Gorki Street
And into Pushkin Square,
Leningrad a rose on the horizon
Ringed by blood and water –
Pull up the blankets
And be small for a few hours of the night.

THE POET

The poet sings his poems on a bridge
A bridge open to horizontal rain
And the steely nudge of lightning,
Or icy moths that bring slow death
Croon him to sleep by snow-wings touching his eyes.

Through this he sings
No people coming close to watch when the snow
Melts and elemental water forces smash
Between cliff and rock under his swaying bridge.
When the water thins, his sweat-drops burst
On scorching rocks like sparks from a flower pod;
Through all this he sits and sings his poems
To those vague crowds on either bank
He cannot make out or consider
With such short sight, for after the first applauded
Poem he let his glasses smash into the rocks below.

The bridge belongs to him, his only property,
Grows no food, supports no houses –
Cheap to buy with the first mediocre poems.
It spans a river that divides two territories –
He knew it and made no mistake:
Today he faces one and tomorrow the other
But from blurred eyes they look the same to him:
Green fields and red-roofed houses
Rising to mountains where wars can be fought
Without a bitter end being reached –
The same on either side.
He does not write a poem every day

But each pet territory takes its turn
To hear his words in one set language burn
And drive them back from each other.

In any rash attack they cannot cross his bridge
But broach the river and ravine
Down at the estuary or far upstream.
He listens to the stunning bloodrush of their arms
And shakes his head, never grows older
As he bends to his paper which one side or the other
Contrives to set, with food, by his hands' reach.
Sometimes sly messengers approach at night
Suggesting he writes and then recites
Upon some momentary theme
To suit one side and damn the other,
At which he nods, tells jokes and riddles
Agrees to everything and promises
That for them he'll tear the world apart
With his great reading.

He stays young, ignoring all requests and prophecies,
But his bridge grows old, the beams and ropes brittle,
And some night alien figures
In a half-circle at each dim bridgehead
Brandish knives and axes. Lanterns flash,
Blades and points spark like spinning moons
Gathering as he puts away pens and parchment,
Closes his eyes, and does not wake for a week,
Knowing he will once more dream
The familiar childhood dream
Of falling down the sheer side of the world
And never wake up.

But he owns and dominates his bridge.
It is his bread and soul and only song —
And if the people do not like it, they can cut him free.

LEFT AS A DESERT

Left as a desert:
Deserted by one great experience
That pulled its teeth and shackles out
And left me as a desert
Under which bones are buried
Over which the sand drifts.

Seven years gone like laden camels:
The gravel and the wind
Is piling this vast desert up
To one sky and one colour
And sky reflecting desert shapes.
The solitary heart lurks on the off-chance
That rain clouds will come and fertilize
The great experience that made this desert.

LOVE IN THE ENVIRONS
OF VORONEZH

Love in the environs of Voronezh
It's far away, a handsome town
But what has it to do with love?
Guns and bombers smashed it down.

Yet love rebuilt it street by street
The dead would hardly know it now
And those who lived forgot retreat.

There's no returning to the heart:
The dead to the environs go
Away from resurrected stone.

Reducible to soil and snow
They hem the town in hard as bone:
The outer zones of Voronezh.

GOODBYE KURSK

The thin moon sliced the heart out as it fell,
Then effortlessly made its way
To the earth's true middle:
The only cure is to fall in love.
The moon gives back what it takes away.

Blocks of flats blot out the moon.
People live with happiness and work;
I left my love too soon, too soon,
So wait for me, it won't seem long.

She put sugar in my coffee
Lit my cigarette
Fed my eyes with the glow of lost desire
Wept when I walked away.

Write to me: it won't seem long.
Hull down: tanks are waiting.
I hear them coming through the dust.

Forests have turned into desert
Powdering the soul to ash,
But sand sends out new blossoms
Till flowers and trees grow strong again.

In the desert that was once a forest
Where eyes see only dust and fire,
Tears dry even as one drinks
On water freely flowing.

Sandgrains fly up nostrils
Turn cool in their protecting flesh,
Salting blood to make a forest
Before the soul can perish.

A brittle seed feeds on the deepest sandgrain
Where the sweated liquid of despair
Makes a forest from the driest desert.

Through a gap in snowlace curtains
Winter turns to fire and sun:
Heat makes the earth a board to spread on
Dust drummed solid by a white sun descending.
Needle-tips tattoo cat-scars on the sky,
Drum-beating letters burn: no escape
From the flat white iron of the sun,
No fauna living but serpent skeletons
Bleached so clean the weakest breath
Can blow such bones as dust.
The white-hot circle blacks out life:
Lie flat and stroke the earth
Before rain comes and rivers overflow.

Hope, a longing for something new,
Crushes the beetle of the past.
When hope takes hold its ruthlessness
Feeds on the purest fuel of injustice,
And sharpens the spike for action.

Whatever you want – bites the fingers.
Be careful what you want:
Wait for the chill river to separate the limits of desire,
For icy banks to break the watercourse
And sweep all venom clean.

Let go, feet tear ladder-rungs
Losing views of pepper dunes
Beyond ampersand trees
In the withered arm of the horizon.
Between the toll of heartsick
Into hole and hiding
The eye of winter's snake-sun
Needles into the heart
Paralyzing both hands to let go.

Life begins when love's game is ended.
Live, and death starts biting:
The game robs you of life.

A week of rain, and the house is an island,
A mudtrack after months of drought
Leads to the paved road.
A smell of spring freshens the brain,
And water slops at the bank as I wade through.

No black sky can finish off the never-ending game,
Or engines drown the memory of peace.

February forty times has arrowed towards spring,
None left behind,
Swirling fish that never vanish,
Colourless or rainbow
Twisting after strange journeys,
Paralyzing vast aquariums.

February is the tunnel's end
A zodiac into soaking loam
When I watch the stars
To say a loud goodbye of welcome to.

Mimosa's dead stench follows like a shadow
Never consumed by the sun
Or swilled by rain,
Rots like memories that went with it.

Be free, and endure happiness –
Summer like a dream from the grave
Rebuilds the heart.
Winter will bring an elegiac falling of the snow
And nurse the purest blossoms –
And green-eyed August
Spread the odour of a wheatfield's death.

Choices bite however the performance.
Scattered seed can bring up crops and flowers
To rub out happiness or suffering.

Midnight comes at any hour.
Eagles out of sunlight bring it,
Shadows on the fields.

The sun throws broken eagles
Back against the stars.
The moon eats and grows fat.

The curtain opens to an empty sky.

LOVERS SLEEP

Flesh to flesh: there are two hearts between us
Mine on one side, yours on the other
Through which all thoughts must pass
Mine intercepting those from you
Yours beating strongly (I feel it doing so)
Taking my thoughts into the labyrinth of yours
From sleep of me to sleep of you
Till flesh and heart join in the deepest cave.

Summer's iron is on the trees
A new weight to bear
Leap-year sap rising through lead
Forcing flower to give fruit
Green flame shifting up iron trunks
To poke out buds.

Leaves hang all summer
Shaken by rain and wind
Shrived by a little heat:
Such yearly swing must wear them
To a death so flat by autumn
That blood draws back
And lets the leaves go.

Trees suffer in frost and snow:
Force-fed by soil, drained by age
They brood and bide their time.
How many summers can they take such weight?
How long is life, how rich the earth,
How weak the heart?

ROSE

A rose about to open
Thinks air and sun
Can turn it into
Something it is not already.

The pink slit of life shows
Between tight green blades –
Hasn't it seen enough
Without wanting everything?

Behind its packed unopened petals
Are roses still to flower
And blossoms not yet dropped;
Outside, those same are tempting it,
Scorched and shrivelled on the grass.
Rose about to open, why do you do it?

What force pushes
So subtly that it does not feel?
What beckoning power beyond
Draws it with perfume sweeter than
The one that will be made?
They promise nothing but the last decay:
The will to come or stay is not their own.

CREATION

God did not write.
He spoke.
He made.
His jackknife had a superblade –
He sliced the earth
And carved the water,
Made man and woman
By an act of slaughter.

He scattered polished diamonds
In the sky like dust
And gave the world a push to set it spinning.
What super-Deity got him beginning
Whispered in his ear on how to do it
Gave hints on what was to be done?

Don't ask.
In his mouth he felt the sun
Spat it out because it burned;
From between his toes – the moon –
He could not walk so kicked it free.

His work was finished.
He put a river round his neck,
And vanished.

SIGNAL BOX

Level-crossing signal box
With three and a half hours between trains.
Bells stopped, gates shut and blocking the line:
Levers taller than himself palisade the moon,
He on the safer side.

Elbows space aside and tunnels
The last green spitter of sparks
Up the stars and soaking turf towards London,
Whispers along, snarling, a retreating song,
Signals on gauges like slicked hair downarrowed:
Line clear for the next open crossing.

Guard in waistcoat and jacket
(Good to children who just want to see)
Iron dragons slip through his fingers a hundred times a day
Responsibility too great to feel power,
Warning others down the line of its approach,
He sits by teaflask and prepares a book,
Needs an opium-portion to become
Captain of a rusting steamer
Crawling the coastal buffs of Patagonia,
Or Nemo in his flying boat
Lording at the Pole or South Sea hideout.
A good tale every night is better
That the telly or a homely bed.

Trains growl on steel snakes
Straight and sleeping close,
Locomotive kings of the dawn
Behind signals from another cured of sleep:
Wide gates open for the first black arrow
A circle in its packed and moving forehead,
As he closes his book
And lets the day pour through.

BARBARIANS

Walls he sat by had fallen long ago:
The city smoked after capture and rapine,
No brick left upon another.

These barbarians – this boy
Sitting on the littered scrub –
Belonged to a Scythian family
Who found the city as if following
A far-back shutter-flash,
Crazed with hope after a famished trudge
Over steppe whose herbs
Scorched by the haze of the sun
Pulled horses' ribs so far in
They were almost dead.
By tale and memory this Scythian offshoot
Saw a glittering metropolis,
People and laden horses queueing to get out.

No brick upon another. While the boy's
Mother scraped at rubbish
He played at tapping stone with stone
Cracked lips moving at the sky
Waiting for her to find food,
And idly placing one brick on another.

SOMME

A trench map from the Battle of the Somme:
Doesn't matter where it came from
Has a dead fly stuck
At the lefthand corner
By a place called Longueval,
Rusty from blood sucked
Out of British or German soldiers
Long since gone over the top
Where many went to in those olden days.

Whoever it was sat on an upturned
Tin and smoked a pipe.
Summer was finished beyond the parapet
And winter not yet willing
To let him through the mist
Of that long valley he was told to cross,
While the earth shook from gnat-bites of gunfire
As if to shrug all men from its shoulders.

A fly dropped on the opened map
Feet of fur and bloated with soot
Crawled over villages he hoped to see.
Bemused he followed it
Curious to know at which point it would stop
And finally take off from,
For that might be
Where death would fall on him.

Scorning the gamble
He squashed the stolid fly
Whose blood now decorates the map
Pinned on my wall after fifty years gone by.

Night came, he counted men into the trench
And crouching on the last day of June
In the earthen slit that stank
Of soil and Woodbines, cordite and shit
Held the wick close to his exhausted eyes,
Shut the dim glow into its case
And ceased to think.

ALCHEMIST

Lead melts. If I saw lead, I melted it
Poured it into sand and made shapes.
I melted all my soldiers,
Watched that rifle wilt
In an old tin can on a gas flame
Like a straw going down
From an invisible spark of summer.
He stood to attention in the tin
Rim gripped by fanatic pliers
From the old man's toolkit,
Looked on by beady scientific eyes
That vandalize a dapper grenadier.

The head sagged, sweating under a greater
Heat than Waterloo or Alma.
He leaned against the side
And lost an arm where no black grapeshot came.
His tired feet gave way,
A spreading pool to once proud groin,
Waist and busby falling in, as sentry-go
At such an India became too hard,
And he lay without pillow or blanket
Never to get up and see home again.

Another one, two more, I threw them in:
These went quicker, an elegant patrol
Dissolved in that infernal pit.
Eyes watering from fumes of painted
Soldiers melting under their own smoke,
The fire with me, hands hard at the plier grip
At soldiers rendered to peaceful lead
At the bottom of a tin.

Swords into ploughshares:
With the gas turned off I wondered
What to do with so much marvellous dead lead
That hardened like the surface of a pond.

VIEW FROM MISK HILL
NEAR NOTTINGHAM

Armies have already met and gone.
When the best has happened
The worst is on its way.
Beware of its return in summer.
When fields are grey and should be green
Rub scars with ash and sulphur.

Full moon clears the land for its own view,
Whose fangs would bereave this field
Of hayrick and sheep.
In the quiet evening birds fly
Where armies are not fighting yet.
He looks a long way on at where he'll walk:
A cratered highway with all hedges gone.

Green land dips and smells of fire.
Topography is wide down there.
The moon waxes and then emaciates.
Birds fatten on fields before migration:
Smoke in summer hangs between earth and sky,
On ground where armies have not fought
But lay their ambush to dispute his passing.

from Snow on the North Side
of Lucifer, 1979

LUCIFER'S ASTRONOMY LESSON

When Lucifer confessed his pride
His plans and turbulence
It was explained to him: the sun
Is fixed in its relation to the stars.
The stars are placed in their position
To each other. The planets with no heat or light
Get sufficient dazzle from the sun.
Satellites enlace the planets.
The earth, with its one moon
Revolves and in so doing
Takes a year to go lefthanded
In a lone ellipse around the fire of Heaven.

And now, a few celestial definitions:
The words came fast, like *nadir*
Zenith, equinox and *solstice,*
But when threatened with *meridian*
And (especially) *declination*
Lucifer shouted: Stop!

I've known this text from birth.
The Guardian of Sidereal Time
Is tired of the Party Line.
Navigators get their fix on *me* –
And so did God.
Right through my heart
The recognition-vectors
Set to split-infinities of Time
Came all too plain yet none too simple,

121

Each emotion a position-line
Pegged like witch-pins in the victim's spleen.
Sextant-eye and timepiece heart
The brain set out in astronomic tables
Plot the way to harbour mouths
Where all life but Lucifer's is understood.

His geologic heart reversed
By extra-galactic longing
Was sensed by God.
Rays leapt from Lucifer's missiled sight:
A magnetic four-way flow
Confused the inner constant,
And mysterious refractions
Made him violent and obstinate,
Shifty and uncouth.
Habits lovable yet also vile
Were ludicrous in minor deities,
Holding mirrors to their chaos.

Handsome though he was, God kicked him out.
Lucifer keened in misery
But in the kernel of his fall
A final sentence frayed his lips:
'God wills everyone to love like him.
In his own image must we love,
Or be stripped bare of everything but space.'

LUCIFER: THE OFFICIAL
VERSION OF HIS FALL

Lucifer once ruled the nations
Till, raddled with perverted notions
He thought to ask God's circling stars
To form a flight of gentle stairs
By which he'd scale the heavenly throne,
Defile it with the rebel stain.
He'd dominate the Mount of Meeting
And silence God's eternal shouting,
Reign a prince in his new birth
Over the outermost poles of the north.

He swore to reach the cloudy peak
And strut on it in God's bright cloak.
He'd speak like God and spout His name
And wave his arms like wings of flame.
He'd rule with cataracts of words,
Keep order among lesser lords;
A universe with rhyme and reason
Would be a mayhem of confusion:
Lucifer control by pride
The gorgeous chaos he bestrode.

But God was neither drunk nor blind
To what Cosmogony had planned.
In his Omnipotence he froze
Restless Lucifer's swirling eyes,
Sent a hundred thousand stars
Hornet-buzzing in vast rays
To drive him mad who thought to try
And take the place of the Most High.
They pinioned him, then made him fall
To the utter depths of Hell.

They tangled him and brought him low.
United Zodiac foresaw
That Lucifer in peace or war
Would be no blessing to their realm.
Faces spurned his rending groan:
Four-point body wheeled and spun
Across the Wilderness of Sin
And struck the cinder of the Sun:
Eternity breeds evolution
And drinks the blood of Revolution.

Declaiming innocence of guile
Yet burned clean of the martyr's role
Lucifer in haughty rancour –
Spewing fire through milky groves –
Condemned the heart of God to canker
And all his satellites as slaves.
Pleas and questions he ignored
In order that the final word
Should stay with him; and then he'd rove
To search for burial and love.

LUCIFER TURNED

Lucifer turned to God and said:
You want my heart, you want my head.
In giving both I'd be your slave.
If only one, I'd bleed to death.
They are as inseparable as breath
That, coming from my mouth, meets ice
And on the stillest air makes smoke.

God did not speak. He never spoke.
Others had to work his throat
And shape such words in their own voice
That God, by silence, made his choice.
But only Lucifer used verse
To save his heart, to save his head –
And still God did not speak or curse
But, spewing cataclysmic gall
Condemned grand Lucifer to fall.

Lucifer slept but once
On the journey south,
For in the morning had to decide
Whether, having crossed the river,
And said goodbye to God
When no more dogs were barking
Nor hut smoke could be seen
Nor any voices heard,
Whether to take the left
Or right arm of the road.

Best not to stop, not think of warmth
But lunge without thought to left or right.
Either that, or broach the centre –
A wilderness of granite-green –
In which one lived as long
And learned far more
Than after the exhaustion of a quick decision
Or the utter ruin of a right one.

UNITY

Memorials being sacred
God made a star of Lucifer
Launched the brilliant morning star
That suited navigators best.

God being what he is
He made another star
The first star of evening
That all women blessed.

They were the hinges of the sky
And never met. One chased,
The other followed. Who did what
Was impossible to test.

Neither wondered who began it,
Trapped as they were, and are,
In the same planet.

NIMROD AND LUCIFER

No one knew why Nimrod shot at the sky.
Such emptiness worked his arms
And sent each arrow whining
Its steep incline at God's power.

Nimrod is a mighty hunter, said the Lord.
Spring was gone. Adonis gored, already
In his furrow, sorrow forgotten,
Wheat whitening a plain too hot for dreams,
The sky blue, God invisible, day vacant,
Animals hiding from the sun.

Lucifer steered each iron point,
But Nimrod was a man, not God:
No feral tip could reach its mark,
Though Mighty Nimrod, wanting God to die,
Wondered why God wasn't dead
And why the arrow fell back from the sky
Anointed with red from notch to tip.

Nimrod wept for shame on seeing
Lucifer's left foot was lame.

THE 'JOB'

The three-decker wooden ship broke its ropes,
Each impacted fibre torn by cobalt water
Lifting its tall stern;

Grating the granite quay
The ship was loose in storm-fists
And no safe harbour locked its arms.

Refuge was in the fang-teeth of the gale
The horizonless ocean
Wood against water
Sails in salty phosphorescence
Mainmast an impaling spike.

The merciless twisting left a hulk
Which Lucifer could not drown:
Not possible for him to know
What made that scabby coffin stay afloat,
Find an unending mirror of water
And merit in God's eye for its long fight.

Progress is an orphan:
Throw a crust it starves to death.
Give it a golden cloak,
A hundred thousand people turn to ash.
Progress either snivels or it kills:
Who owns it holds a sun to limping Lucifer
Who vowed God's rebels harnessed his effulgence
And made galactic storms.

Progress will be the death of me, said God.
Let me turn the notion on its head.
God said: 'Empedocles, say this:
"Progress is the bitch of war;
Love and discord suckle it.
For once I'll speak plain:
War gets the world nearer to death,
Does no one good.
No sane man cares to die a king,
Or idiot become a god."'

Empedocles simplified, and got it wrong:
'War is the father of progress' –
Then simpered in his golden sandals
To Etna's hot volcanic rim
Wondering whether God was right
To give such force the name of war.

Lucifer smiled. Empedocles stood close,
Peered into the boiling din.
'Your question has no answer,' said Lucifer,
And pushed him in.

LUCIFER THE ARCHER

Robin Hood's light-hearted men
In Sherwood Forest shot
At silver pennies marked
With a silver cross.

Lucifer, toxophilite,
Tipped the arrows true,
Drew back every archer's yew
With fingers of Sherwood green.

Thus, fletched missiles overseen
Found numismatic tracks –
God's son or not, the cross was shot
By Lucifer's speeding sticks.

When two lines met
And, meeting, crossed,
And closed themselves in a ring
Lucifer felt a prison clang

Around his brow and through his eyes –
So made the outlaws' arrows smash
Against all silver pennies
That bore a silver cross.

LUCIFER AND COLUMBUS

Lucifer became the sun:
Drew Christopher Columbus on
Into oceanic dusk.

Under the basin of the night
They followed stars
He patterned in their track.

By morning Lucifer arose
And deigned to push them over
The daily fortitudes of dawn.

The navigator's cross-stays
Angled him
To guess the distance of the day.

When the fathom-line was flung
Its lead-head hit the sea and burst
In Lucifer's fluorescent sparks.

He steadied the flickering needle
Through the Sargasso Sea,
Goaded a meteor to perform

A spectacular welcome,
And lured the Sons of Adam
Back to Paradise.

Lucifer the surveyor didn't look
He measured, hands performing
A theodolite not prayer.

A dot behind the eyes held cosmography
In thrall, geometry intuition as he spanned
Paced and taped a kingdom in a day
Triangulated oceans in one night.

God took the credit
Every action in the world was His,
All seas and continents. He led

Footsteps on and filled all hearts
A wind banging the canvas sails
Of a ship whose crew was drunk
On loot, lewdness and the Lord.

Rejected Lucifer was bruised
Since science followed him not God.
He melted raw materials, lay rails, grew cities

Rolled lightning in a drum and made it work.
Adam's sons ripped milk and honey from the earth
And God was praised.
But Lucifer saw his limp on every foot.

LUCIFER THE MECHANIC

Lucifer invented speed, taught
That one slow pulley drives a fast,
A sluggish stream revolves a mill
How fire melts and wind shifts
And iron floats and alloys fly.

Lucifer's willing scholars learned
How one metal cuts another
And steel spread on a spindle
Is in its weakness flaked
By a stilled blade set against it.

A lubricated drill-tip
Tempered to diamond strength
Spins to steel clamped in a jig:
By playing speed to altered speed
Steel teeth in a circle
Mill into a shank of steel.

Lucifer in every lathe
Manufactured objects beyond
Man's vulnerable version of himself;
He unmade God, and at his most demonic
Turned Man into an industrious mechanic.

LUCIFER AND REVOLUTION

When workers assembled at the station
Lucifer had waited since the swamp was drained.
Jutting chin and jaunty cap and posh Swiss overcoat,
Finger stabbing the air to rights,
He licked his Tartar lips and stroked
His beard, nodding sharply
At each injustice he would cure,
Clipped decisive words in steam-train language
Knit the crowd into carded fabric
Any pattern could be printed on.

He had waited long for such deep cheers
And smoky mosaic of faces,
Dimmed his eyes to just the right amount
Of inability to see the future,
When the mob would do such deeds
As burned all sensibility to ash:

'Oh boy, we did that fucking castle in!
Splintered every lintel, broke every brick.
Those Old Masters burned a treat.
Forty years ago the duke raped my mother
So I plugged his duchess-daughter.
For the Revolution, of course –
We should have one every day!'

The shock-detachment of the Revolution came
Behind a glistening array of guns:
'All right, chaps, fun's over.
You work for us now, what?

So build that castle up again.
And who was that swine raped the duchess?
His trial starts tomorrow.'

'The purity of Revolution shines
Bright for all to see,
A moral force that cleanses
Cleaner than the sea.'

'You'll be sorry you spoke,'
Comrade Lucifer retorted
When everything got out of hand.
'You helped to make the Revolution,
Now you'll be voted to the wall
Or destitution unimaginable.
I'm not Hamlet lost for a yes or no.
I'll make an omelette any day
And break as many eggs as there are heads.
Chickens lay all the time!'
His grin was geological – under the moustache.

The assassin's bullet didn't kill
But scared him. He vanished.
Only One could play that game and win.

LUCIFER TELEGRAPHIST

Lucifer, God's listener,
Took telegrams in any code
Or language, heard

    the blissful separation
    of those who would never touch again

    the marriage of a thousand needles
    knitting both victims till death

    the assault of a new mouth
    soon to connive at the smash of nations

    the frantic beggary of save-our-souls
    when a ship's parts separate in revenge
    on those who ripped wood and iron
    from the generous soil

    communiqués that order war
    when other greeds have failed.

Happiness and agony went through his heart,
God's ears not enough.
He wanted power to end all suffering
And call it peace.

Rebellion failed. Robbed of God's favour
Lucifer sat in universal grief
So that his Fall was liberation.

138

HYMN TO LUCIFER

Lucifer is the True God:
Not the God of Man
Or the God of God
But the God of Light.

Luminous of eyes
Limitless of sight
A thousand million miles
Are his to roam.

Ice is no prison
Fire no opposite,
The sun a cool exit
To spaces beyond.

The earth's inferno-centre
Cannot hold him,
Nor galactic spaces
Lose him.

Newton did not go to church;
He hardly ever went to chapel:
He read Maimonides in bed
And pondered on the fallen apple.

The Board of Admirals agreed
That the first chronometer of Harrison
Was in spite of its complexity and size
Accurate beyond comparison.

Enigmatic Einstein vowed
He'd see the hardy atom burst:
The world would shrivel to a cell
If Germany achieved it first.

God concurred, yet did not know
What the first flash would do to Him.
Lucifer hoped that God might die
When that smoke-hill hit the sky.

Lucifer's simple scheme was to kill God
And create another
And after mutual annihilation
Crow the victor from their ashes –
Once they cooled.

Every plotter is naive, every planner blind:
On a calm and August morning
The boil burst.
The sea was in it and the sky
The centre of the earth took part
The sun and moon looked on
And thus participated. A particle
Of every man woman child
And other creature
That had been on earth since earth began
Will be remembered for connivance –
Lucifer made sure of that.

The sun went cool to let
This fiery flood of Lucifer-vomit
Like a cauliflower fist
Deal a belly-blow to God.

Scorched and broken
Lucifer fell back,
And wept.

Lucifer met Job.
He saw flame
He touched fire
But could not get close.

Endurance is a herb
The flame protects.
The sun comes
The sun goes –

Job spoke:
A flame lives on
In darkness.
Nor is it extinguished
By the sun.

LUCIFER AND NOAH

Noah believed,
Built his boat
Called his creatures
Two by two;

Lucifer watched
The floating city
On the flood,
Could not help
Hands whose fingers
Spread before they sank.

The void world
Was life for Lucifer.
He ruled a sea of corpses –
Yet welcomed Noah
Ashore at Ararat.

LUCIFER AND DANIEL

Seven famished lions
Circled Daniel
In Babylon's oblivion-hole;

Eyes in darkness
Were the king's prisoners
And only Daniel's
Emitted light.

Your eyes hunger
Daniel spoke
But my hunger
Is greater.

The lions paced, bewildered,
As if Daniel's flesh was bitter
And God his fearlessness.

Since his Fall
Lucifer had never been so close.

Lucifer tramped from sea to sea,
Burning grit pained every step
An island moving through the land
From Carmel to the Mount of Moses.

Lucifer paid his forty days,
His flesh bled gravel
In the sleepless cool of the night,
Gypsum and alabaster glowed at the moon:
Although I fell
Although you threw me to the heathens
Although you scattered me among
The far stars of the universe;
Moulded me in ice, let heat dissolve me,
Melted me in fire, let ice find me,
My day is at hand, and the effect of every vision.
Say to me where my sanctuary is,
Scatter me back up the galactic chimney of the Fall.

Lucifer walked between crimson cliffs
Found garnets in the soil that matched
The stone embedded in his forehead
Scooped them to the foldings of his cloak
And walked another forty days.
Granite islands glistened in vast seas of sand.
The mountains of Arabia were blue:
The effect of every vision was at hand.

The Sinaitic wind beyond Ophir
Cleaned shattered tanks and guns.
Lucifer pressed the metal that his fire had holed and melted,
A camel rooted thorns between the wheels.
When dark drew on to Egypt
The effect of every vision was at hand.

Lucifer was the mirror of God's pride
Until his vanity
Created
Infamous
Fractures
Ending his reign yet marking his
Return to God.

Infamy
Stems

From believing pride to be
One's possession, which sets you to
Retaliate against the weals of fate.
God has no pride. Lucifer's mistake
In thinking so was responsible for the
Vanquishing of
Entire
Nations.

THE LAST

When God said
Let there be Man
He also said
Let there be Lucifer.

Lucifer became
And in becoming
Was the only threat to God.

Lucifer is part of God
And part of Man:
Unity is limitless
Small and indivisible.

Lucifer thought
God ruled through Lucifer
But God rules alone.
Man rules, if and when,
Through Lucifer.

Lucifer walks in circles,
With God forever present
And forever silent.

GOODBYE LUCIFER

Goodbye, Lucifer, goodbye:
I say goodbye to everything;
When the end arrives and knocks its time
My body won't dictate the tune
Nor my soul sing dead.
Goodbye, Utopia
Whose minute never came.
Goodbye –
In case I cannot say it then
Or death's too slow for me to care.

Goodbye, Lucifer, goodbye
People music language maps
Goodbye to love
And rivers alluvially curving.
Goodbye the sky.

Goodbye, Lucifer and all reflections,
Farewell to bodies and machinery
Goodbye the spirit of the universe
Goodbye.

from Sun Before Departure,
1974–1982

HORSE ON
WENLOCK EDGE

A tired horse treads
The moonpocked face
Of a ploughed field

Cuts furrows blindly
Through drifting rain
On chestnut trees, soaked hedges

Energy sucked out with evening;
Seven nails in each steel shoe
Are empty scars of twenty-eight nights

When the white horse dreams
Of galloping through star-clouds,
A moon of nails flying from its path.

Clouds play with their water
Distort shekels between grass
Enriched by the city that flattens
Surrounding land with rubbish;

Binoculars ring the distance like a gun:
From a sea of shining slate
Churches lift and chimneys lurch,
Modern blocks block visions,

The Robin Hood Rifles drilled in fours
Practised azimuths on far-off points,
Eyes watering at southern hills
A half-day's march away:

'They'll have to swim the Trent, thou knows,
God-damn their goldfish eyes!'
Musket balls rush, break glass,
Make rammel. The Nottingham Lambs

Smashed more than a foreign army,
Came through twitchells to spark the rafters
Paint pillars with the soot of anarchy.
The Trent flowed in its scarlet coat

Too far off to deal with fire:
The council got our Castle in the end
Protected by Captain Albert Ball VC
Who thrust into a cloud-heap above Loos

Hoping for his forty-second kill.
In school they said: 'You're born
For Captain Albert Ball
To be remembered. Otherwise he'd die!'

A private soldier, he became Icarus:
'Dearest Folks, I'm back again
In my old hut. My garden's fine.
This morning I went up, attacked five Huns

Above the Line. Got one, and forced two down
But had to run, my ammunition gone.
Came back OK. Two hits on my machine.'
Fate mixed him to a concrete man

An angel overlooking
On the lawn of Nottingham's squat fort.
My memory on the terrace
Remembers barges on the Leen

Each sail a slice of paper, writing
Packed in script of tunic-red.
For eighteen years I blocked the view
No push to send me flying.

Another brain shot down in sleep:
Rich Master Robin Hood outside the walls
Where he belongs robs me of time
And does not give it to the poor.

The whimsical statue stood
With hat and Sherwood weapons
Till a Nottingham Lamb removed the arrow
Someone later nicked the bow

Then they stole the man himself
And rolled his statue down the hill
One football Saturday
And splashed it in the Trent:

If you see it moving, take it:
If it doesn't move, steal it bit by bit
But do not let it rest till Death's sonic boom
Blows the sun through every Castle room.

OXNEY

Smoke all evening, too thin to move
Stubble aflame
Up a hillside when I drove
Across the flat half-mile between

Iden and the Isle of Oxney. A line
Of white, lipped in red set a corner
Of the battlefield on fire,
And cloud like a grey cloak was pulled along

By some heart-broken mourner going home.

NORTH STAR ROCKET

At the North Pole everywhere is south.
Turn where you will
Polaris in eternal zenith
Studs the world's roof.

Under that ceiling
A grey rocket crosses
A continent of ice,
Evading Earth by flirting with it.

Who will know what planet he escaped from?
A cone of cosmic ash pursued its course
On automatic pilot set to earth

Bringing Death – or a new direction
To be fed into my brain
Before collision.

FIFTH AVENUE

A man plays bagpipes on Fifth Avenue.
Gaelic-wail stabbing at passersby
Who wish its pliant beckoning
Would draw them through their fence of discontent
To a field of freedom they can die in.
They stand, and then walk on.

A man with thick grey beard
Goes wild between traffic,
Arms wagging semaphore;
Raves warnings clear and loud
To those ignoring him.

A blind man rattles a money-can,
Dog flat between his legs
Listens to the demanding
Tin that has so little in
Both ears register
Each bit that falls.

An ambulance on a corner:
They put a man on a stretcher
Who wants air. A woman says:
'Is it a heart-attack?
Is the poor guy dead?'
She worries for him:
Dying is important when it comes.

'I suppose it is,' I guess,
'I hope it's not too late' –
She had one last year:
'Fell in the street, just like that.'
Her lips move with fear.
The man is slid into the van.

Just like that.
Hard to come and harder go
For the bagpipe player in the snow
The wild man with his traffic sport
The old man with his dog
And the young who hurry:
Dying, a lot of it goes on.

THE LADY OF BAPAUME

There was a lady of Bapaume
Whose eyes were colourless and dead –
Until the falling sun turned red;
Her lovers from across the foam
Walked at dawn towards her bed:
Fell in fields and sunken lanes
Died in chalk-dust far from home.

A rash of scattered poppy-stains:
Nowadays they pass her wide –
That mistress of *chevaux-de-frise*
Is still alive and can't conceal
Her mournful and erotic zeal:
The lady of Bapaume had charms –
Bosom large, but minus arms.

No soldiers rise these days and go
Towards the bloodshot indigo.
Motorways veer by the place
On which, with neither love nor grace,
They drive to holidays in Spain.
There was a lady of Bapaume
Whose lovers ate the wind and rain.

Names fade,
Suave air of Picardy erodes
The regimental badge
Or cross
Or David's Star
Of gunner this and private that.
The chosen captains and their bombardiers
And those known but as nothing unto God
Who brought them out of slime and clay
Are taken back again.

God knew each before they knew themselves
If ever they did
Before mothers lips sang
Brothers showed
Sisters taught
Fathers put them out to school or work.
But only God may know them when the stones are gone
If any can –
If God remembers what God once had done.

AUGUST

Birth, the first attack, begins at dawn.
It's also the last, whistle at sky-fall,
Illogical, unsynchronized, inept.
Children, pushed over the top
And kettledrummed across churned furrows
Kitted out with dreams and instinct,
Hope to learn before reaching the horizon.
Those in front call back advice:
'Going to advance, send reinforcements.'
But who trust the old, when they as young
Spurned cautionary wisdom
That never harmonized with youth?
'Going to a dance, send three-and-fourpence.'

Some fall quietly under each rabid burst of shell
Love of life unnoticed
In willingness to give it
Or the feckless letting-go.
Leaves drop in the zero-hour of spring
Young heat mangled by car or motorbike.

Broken sight looks in, no view beyond
Though terror rocks the heart to sleep
The signal-sky gives bad advice:
Get up, look outside, day again.
Insight warped by energy, blinded by ignorance.

The battlefield too wide,
Bullets rage at friends and parents
Strangers stunned in the lime-pits of oblivion.
Who blame for this sublime attack?
Did Brigadier-General God in his safe bunker plan?
He horsebacks by, devoted cheers.
Choleric face knows too much to tell –
It's dangerous for any smile to show.
Whoever is cursed must be believed in
For Baal is dead. Get up. Push on.
Want to live forever?
Go through. No psychic wound can split
Or leg be lost at that onrushing slope.

Halfway, more craven, sometimes too clever,
Old campaigners want a hole to flatten in
Before rot of the brain encircles
Or Death's concealed artillery
Plucks fingers from the final parapet.
Silence kills as quickly, you can bet.
Live on. Death pulls others in
Not you, or me, or us (not yet).

Earth underfoot is kind but waiting,
Green sea flows on the right flank,
Black rain foils the leftward sun,
Poppy clouds and mustard fields
Tricked out with dead ground, full woods,
Lateral valleys flecked with cornflowers.
Roses flake their fleshy petals down.
Time falls away. Battle deceptively recedes,
Peace lulls to the final killing ground,
Familiar voices coming up behind.

TERRORIST

The protest against Death
Is a raised fist, the face
Of corruption bewails its declining
Gift of life. I go when chosen for taking.
The sky bruises the aching fist. Air mellows
The corroded face. You did not choose me.
I parted myself long ago when I sat
On a branch overlooking boathouse
And bulrushes, and the lake water
On which nothing moved
Except the breath of words
Saying no seven times all told.
I didn't stay to hear the answer
Turned blind in Death's donkey-circle
Till the rag around my fist
Was bloodsoaked from hitting the trees.

RABBIT

A busy rabbit young and small
Cornered our vegetable plot,
Chewing green treasure,
Tail upright from line to line
In rabbit-fashion,
An all-providing God set out
Row on row of grub,

Scarpered back to thistles
Till heavy-treading vengeance went away.

The fur-lined malefactor fed a fortnight
On lettuce carrots peas,
Slyly keeping news from friends below.

Laden gun half-aimed, I stalked:
That gorging salad-engine's tender paws
Which sensed the weight of lead shot in my pocket,
And soft-footed off before I reached the hedge.

My shadow half-close,
Approaching blackout had low odds
On lead-slug hitting his well-padded neck.

It never did
Though if that produce had been all
Between us and hunger
The senses would have sharpened
And my gun been God Almighty.

MOTH

Drawn by the white glitter of a lamp
A slick-winged moth got in
My midnight room and ran quick
Around the switches of a radio.

Antennae searched the compact powerpacks
And built-in aerials, feet on metal paused
At METER-SELECT, MINIMUM-MAX
TUNER, VOLUME, TONE
Licked up shortwave stations onto neat
Click-buttons with precision feet.

Unable to forego the next examination
My own small private moth seemed all
Transistor-drunk on fellow-feeling,
A voluptuous discovery pulled
From some far bigger life.
A thin and minuscule antenna
Felt memory backtuning as it crawled
Familiar mechanism, remembering an instrument
Once cherished,
Forgotten but loved for old times' sake.

I switched the wireless on, and the moth
To prove its better senses
Mocked me with open wings and circled the light,
Making its own theatre, which outran all music.

FISHES

Fishes never change their habits:
A million years seem like a day
As far as fishes' habits go.

Beware of those who change them half as fast
Like people every year or so
So fast you cannot find
A firm limb or settled eye.

The constancy of fishes is unique.
They multiply but keep their habits
In deep and solitary state;

Feel unique and all alone
Not being touched and hardly touching
Even to keep the species spreading –
Unique is never-changing habits.

Fishes are flexible and fit the water,
And though continually moving
Never change their habits.

THISTLES

Thistles grow in spite of flowers,
Brittle taproots drawing succour till the autumn.

Seeds flop from the hedge
And at puberty suck their fill by beans and carrots.

Entrenching blade hacks soil,
And fingers under thistle-spikes grip,

And easily out it's tossed to the sun's bake.
A dry and useless thistle pricks –

Fingers gather and inflate with pus:
For weeks the memory of pain.

RELEASE

Flowers wilt, leaves feloniously snatched,
Birds sucked away – autumn happens.
Frenetic bluebottles saw the air.
Blackberries scratch with poison.

Love is taken before knowing the mistake.
The last thief grins
At the look of life.
There are many, so who cares?

The trap is a loaded crossbow,
Ratchet-pulley sinewed back
From birth and set in wait.
None walk upright from the bolt's release.

LEFT HANDED

The left hand guards my life.
I use. It uses. Sinister
Alliances shape plans.

Left hand is fed by the heart
Strategically engined
Between brain and fingers,
Sometimes filtering intelligence.

The left eye is in line with hand
And pen. The left lung
Rotted when I tried the right:
Lesson one was spitting blood.

Vulnerable left side lives in harmony
And liberates the rules,
Rides monsters who fear to eat themselves,
So do not bite.

NEW MOON

Since men have waved flags on her
Classified geology with peacock colours
Sent cameras probing every angle
The moon has turned lesbian;

Shows brighter now in her woman hunger
Goes with purpose to her lover
In the Milky Way, nothing more from earth

Yet better by far than shining palely
A mirror for courtiers to gawp at –
And that stricken poet who ached
In her unrequiting love but now is free.

OPHELIA

When Ophelia lay a finger on the water
The cold and shallow brook scorched flesh.
She pulled it back.

The fire was love.
She was forget-me-not's daughter,
Each eye a pond of flowers.

She climbed the arching cliff
Where water sent its clouds of salt,
Luminous across the sun.

The nunnery was found:
No one saw her body spin.
A lunar sea-change sent it cleanly in.

ALIOTH THE BIGOT

A bigot walks fast.
Get out of the way
Or walk faster.

He walked faster too
Veered right
To evade me.

I increased my rate
Hinging left to avoid
The fire in his eyes.

Collisionable material
Should not promenade
On the same street.

We muttered sorry
Then went on
More speedily than ever.

Down the slope to the horizon
Fix the black-dot sun before departure.
When the day sets at the storm's end
Far along the moonbeams that flow in,
Shut the barometer, hang the watch away
Lay the sextant in its box.

How deep the valley which enclosed
The lifeboat washed against the shore.
The heart says goodnight at dawn,
And hopes the dark is best
Which fears the day to come.

The way to knowing is to know
How useless to talk of hills and colours
Looking at Jerusalem.

To know is to keep silent
Yet in silence
One no longer knows;

Can never unknow what was known
Or let silence slaughter reason.
One knows, and always knows

Unable to believe silence
A better way of knowing.
One sees Jerusalem, knows

Yet does not, comes to life
And knows that walls outlast whoever watches.
The Temple was destroyed: one knows for sure.

One joins the multitude and grieves.
Knows it from within.
One does not know. Let me see you

Everyday as if for the first time
Then I'll know more:
Which already has been said

By wanderers who, coming home,
Regret the loss of that first vision.
The dust that knew it once is mute.

Stones that know stay warm and silent.
From pale dry hills I watch Jerusalem,
Make silence with the stones:
An ever-new arrival.

NAILS

Tel Aviv is built on sand:
Sand spills from a broken paving stone
And sandals cannot tread it back;

Waves beat threateningly
A sea to flow through traffic
Climb hills and wash Jerusalem.

Every white-eyed speckle of its salt
Feasts on oranges and people,
Envying their safety;

And their rock through which
Six million nails were hammered
As deep as the world's middle,
And the sky that no floodtide can reach.

LEARNING HEBREW

With coloured pens and pencils
And a child's alphabet book
I laboriously draw
Each Hebrew letter
Right to left
And hook to foot,
Lamed narrow at the top,
The steel pen deftly thickening
As it descends
And turns three bends
Into a black cascade of hair,
Halting at the vowel-stone
To one more letter.

Script comes up like music
Blessing life
The first blue of the sea
The season's ripe fruit
And the act of eating bread:
Each sign hewn out of rock
By hands deserving God as well as Beauty.

I'm slow to learn
Cloud-tail shapes and whale-heads
Arks and ships in black, pure black
The black of the enormous sky
From behind a wall of rock:
With their surety of law
Such shapes make me illiterate
And pain the heart

As if a boulder bigger than the earth
Would crush me:
Struck blind I go on drawing
To enlighten darkness.

Such help I need:
Lost in this slow writing,
Clutch at a letter like a walking-stick
Go into the cavern-mouth
And sleep by phosphorescent letters
Dreaming between *aleph* or *tav*
Beginning and end
Or the lit-up middle.

Dreams thin away:
In day the hand writes
Hebrew letters cut in my rock
Painted by a child on the page,
For they are me and I am them
But can't know which.

SYNAGOGUE IN PRAGUE

Killers said
Before they used their slide-rules
'Death is the way to Freedom':
Seventy-seven thousand names
Carved on these great walls
Are a gaol Death cannot open.

Eyes close in awe and sorrow
As if that name was my mother
That boy starved to death my son
Those men gassed my brothers
Or striving cousins.

It might have been me and if it was
I spend a day searching the words
For my name.
I'd be glad it was not me
If the dead could see sky again,
Reach that far-off river and swim in it.

What can one say
When shouting rots the brain?
The dead god hanging in churches
Was not allowed to hear
Of work calling for revenge
To ease the pain of having let it happen
And stop it being planned again.

Letters calling for revenge on such a wall
Would vandalize that encyphered synagogue,
And seventy-seven thousand
Stonily indented names
Would still show through.

Vengeance is Jehovah's own;
To prove He's not abandoned us
He gave the gift of memory,
The fruit of all trees
In the Land of Israel.

ISRAEL

Israel is light and mountains
Bedrock and river
Sand-dunes and gardens,
Earth so enriched
It can be seen from
The middle of the sun.

Without Israel
Would be
The pain
Of God struck from the universe
And the soul falling
Endlessly through night.

Israel
Guards the Sabbath-candle of the world
A storm-light marking
Job's Inn – open to all –
An ark without lifeboats
On land's vast ocean.

ON AN OLD FRIEND
REACHING JERUSALEM

No one may ask what I am doing here:
Olive-leaves one side glisten tin
The other is opaque like my dulled hair.
I travelled far. I walked. I ate
The train's black smoke,
Choked on Europe's bitter sin.

When forests grew from falling ash
I gleaned the broken letters of my alphabet
And sucked them back to life for bread.
Christian roofs were painted red
And four horizons closed their doors.

Pulled apart by Europe's sky
My soul is polished by Jerusalem
Where I fall fearlessly in love
Ashen by the Western Wall,
And through my tears no one dare ask
What I am doing here.

FESTIVAL

The moon came up over Jerusalem
Blood-red
An hour later it was white
Bled to death.

The breath of memory revives
On the Fifteenth Day of Ab.
The spirit and the flesh
Don't clash when men and women
Walk in orange groves
To reinvigorate the moon.

God knew the left hand
And the right
When Lot chose
The Plain of Ha-Yarden
And Abram – Canaan.

An excruciating noise of car brakes
Comes from the Valley of Hinnom.
Jerusalem is ours.

YAM KINNERET
(THE SEA OF GALILEE)

Galilee is a lake of reasonable size,
Unless immensity is measured down
In dreams, in darkness.
Then it becomes an ocean.

Distant sails are birds trapped
On the unreflecting surface,
As if savage fish below
Pull at their wings.

With casual intensity
And such immensity
Are new dreams made from old.

EZEKIEL

On the fifth day
In the fourth month
Of the thirtieth year
Among the captives by the river
A storm wind came out of the north.
Ezekiel the priest saw visions:

Saw Israel
Had four faces
Four wings
Four faces:

The face of a man
The face of a lion
The face of an ox
The face of an eagle.

That was the vision of Ezekiel.

THE ROCK

Moses drew water from a cliff.
I set my cup
Till it was filled.

Water saved me, and I drank,
Reflecting on
The shape of flame

Of how a fire needs
Putting down
By swords of water.

IN ISRAEL,
DRIVING TO THE DEAD SEA

I drive a car. Cars don't
Figure much in poems.
Poets do not like them,
Which is strange to me.

Poets do not make cars
Never have, not
One nut or bit of Plexiglass
Passes through their fingers.

No reason why they should.
To make a bolt or screw
Is not poetic. To fit a window:
Is that necessary?

Likewise an engine
Makes a noise. It smells,
And runs you off too fast.
What's more you have to sit

As fixed at work as that
Engine-slave who made it.
Nevertheless I drive a car
With pleasure. It makes my life poetic

I float along and tame
The road against all laws
Of nature. I stay alive.
Who says a poet shouldn't drive

On a highway which descends so low
Yet climbs so high
From Jerusalem to Jericho?

EIN GEDI

(After Shirley Kaufman's essay: 'The Poet and Place')

When David went from Jerusalem
The itch of death was in the air.
The salt sea bloomed.
King Saul bit himself and followed.
The cave had no windows to steam and view.
David's gloom was David's soul, and hid him.

Whether to go or stay became
A cloak that fitted when he went.
After the mournful grackle's note
Saul came searching for the kill
But never felt the sword that cut his cloak.
Darkness is our place.
The cave gave David birth:
Memory was born, and all his songs.

EVE

In Israel I looked out of the window
And saw Eve.

Her hair was so black
I called her Midnight
But no answer came.

Her eyes were amber
Jewels made at midday
When she looked at me.

She crossed Gehenna
In her sandals.
My daylight wanted her,

A few-minute love-affair
Lasted forever,
As she entered her City.

from Tides and Stone Walls,
1986

RECEDING TIDE

The tide is fickle.
After going out it comes back.
The moon sees to that.

It's what the tide reveals
When it huffs and leaves
That means so much,

And what the tide covers
On nibbling back
That opens our eyes:

Archipelagos left unexplored
And rivers unsurveyed:
But before the meaning's known

The regimental rush of waves
Is preceded by
The brutal skirmishing of dreams.

BRICKS

Bricks build walls
They erect homes
Both rise up
Men make them out of earth and clay.
Water tightens them
Ovens bake them to withstand
Bullets and dour weather.

Rectilinear and hard
Red or blue
Porous or solid
Beautifully stacked:
They invite the mason's hand
To choose.

Bombs are the enemy of bricks:
Stroke them tenderly,
And share their warmth.

LANDSCAPE –
SENNEN, CORNWALL

How many died when the height was taken?
Upslope the armoured horses went:
Old refurbished iron-men
Zig-zagging from rocks,
And knights already fallen.

The cunning defenders
Jabbed soft underbellies,
Brought riders down
On gleaming daggers.

Victors mourned
As the defeated King rode
Into rain beyond the hill.

Blood makes history,
And desolation
A winter's day.

BOARDED-UP WINDOW

If I rip these planks back
Will I see
Something new, or out of nature?

Years ago I put them on
Felt glee in my fist
As I swung the hammer
And saw each nail
Biting into seasoned wood.

I didn't know what I boarded up:
Sunlight on the beach
Pebbles in my palms
Grass in my teeth –
An upturned rowing boat.

Thumb and forefinger held the nail.
I laughed at something new
Or out of nature.
They paid me – though not too well.

If I have the strength (or tools)
To lever off those planks
My soul will dazzle me with grief,
And out of my own nature blind me
With what I boarded up.

DERELICT BATHING CABINS
AT SEAFORD

Well, they would, wouldn't they?
They'd say anything.
Doris and Betty got undressed.
Bob and Fred did the same next door.
The things that went on in these changing huts.
Well, with the War over, what could you expect?
They came back like new men.
Well, they came back.
They came, anyway.
Sometimes it was you and my Fred.
Then it might be me and your Bob.
It was nice with us, though, wasn't it?
Nothing but a clean bit of fun.
Sad they went in a year of each other –
The dirty devils!
Nothing but a clean bit of fun,
When we changed into our costumes,
The sea washed it off, though, didn't it?
We had some good swims as well.
And now look how they've smashed 'em up.
Poor old bathing huts.
Never be the same again.
The sea chucked all them pebbles in.
Don't suppose it liked the goings-on.
Then the vandals ripped the doors off.
They didn't like it, either.

Old times never come back,
But at least we 'ad 'em!

SOUTHEND PIER

A pier is a bridge that failed,
You might say –
Whatever else is said.

At the end are fish, and ships,
And underneath is water,
Or jewelled shingle.

Lamp posts point to the signal station
So does the toytown railway.
People buy and sell.

The planks smell fresh.
Not liking salt
They reach for land.

A rotund father and thin daughter
Stroll hand in hand.
Good for business.

A walking-stick clatters
But don't look now:
The invisible man goes by.

Every pier has one.
He swaggers to the end and back,
Panama hat at an angle;

And then again returns,
Craving land beyond the water,
Wound-up to walk forever.

DERELICT HOUSES
AT WHITECHAPEL

We came off the ship:
'This is America. We're here!'
A shorter crossing
Than the railway trip.
Having to make a living
Was better than in Russia.
Nobody tried to kill us.

America was smaller than we thought.
We lived three generations
In those houses:
New Year
Atonement
Passover.

Bricks talk,
But Books are eloquent.

AFTER A ROUGH SEA,
AT SEAFORD

He went to sea because he didn't like the dark.
He wanted his ship to be looked at from the shore
By a woman who would wonder
Where he was going and why
But not where coming from:
His mother;

And stared at by a man who envied him
And craved to follow:
His father.

Many do not like the dark
But on a ship at night the lights stay on
Inside yourself.
You take it like a mother into you
In case the sun won't show at dawn.

At sea there's only
Space, and you.

After thirty years he came home.
He had forgotten the house
But recognized the window.

His sister never married
But she knew he'd come.
They passed unknowing in The Lanes.

The first iron dewdrop of the knocker
Shook dust
From the flowers.

'Not today!' she said.
He walked away,
Forgot the house

Forgot the window
Forgot his sister never married
Forgot the knocker made no sound

When it struck home.

The Big Voice, the Visual Scream
Shouts about the National Lottery
Or the advantage of travelling by Aeroflot
Or the holiness of the Virgin's Grotto
Or a film about the antics
At the court of King Otto;
Or did someone win
A Motto Competition –
First prize a reproduction
On a theme by Watteau?

Or, taking it all in all (and altogether)
Let's have a scenario like this:
The Big Bang Lottery Prize
Is a trip by Aeroflotto
To the Virgin's Grotto
In a corner of the Empire
Of mad King Otto –
From which you come back, if at all
(You've guessed it) BLOTTO;
Crossing the frontier in a haycart
Concealed inside the wrappings
Of a Cracker Motto
Against an idealized backdroppo
As designed by Watto.

Speculation is a dead-end,
So forget it. A mindless hand
A single rip: we'll never know
Where poster-dreams
And demons that lurk behind them go.

New Poems, 1986–1990

CAMOUFLAGE

In winter trees don't move:
Half the lawn is coppered with leaves,
Scollops under the bare trees.

A snow-blue sheet, no sky:
A ginger cat from copper into green
Stalks careless birds.

Can't tell when it reaches bushes,
Form and colour blending
For its survival.

DAWN PIGEON

Below,
Cars slide on macadam tracks
Called streets.

Almost a circle,
Vision pauses to detect
A winter warning from the east.

People
Clatter towards train and bus,
Traffic a departing Joseph-scarf.

Vibrations shiver up the slates
To aerial filigree of bars
For webbed feet to grip.

No rival dare approach
His view of dustbins
Under blistered sills.

Well-fed and grey,
Lord as much as can be done
From his high perch –

Swoops when he decides to go,
Down, not up,
A common pigeon of the Town.

Claptrap, I said. Don't like this school.
Or probably much worse. If I'd learned
Nothing else I cursed like a sailor.
But five years old. Yet good, as good as gold.
They think I'm a fool?
Why am I here? They can say what they like.
They show me the swimming pool.
I get pushed in. It's cold.
My arms ache. I hold the bar,
Then aim for the other side. Not far.

Definitely don't like it. Suck my thumb.
Don't suck your thumb!
Scratch my nose. Don't do that!
She tells about The Wooden Horse of Troy.
Even I wouldn't have hauled that toy
Through the city walls like that.

She gives out bricks. We have to build.
Two suns blind her glasses.
Build, she says, build!
So I build a town. It gets knocked down.
Shall I throw them? Watch that frown.

She reads of Abraham from the Bible.
God says: Tie your son up on a pile of stones
Then slit his throat to show you love me most.
Isaac doesn't like it but his father
Lifts the knife. Just in time God tells him: Stop!
I believe you now, so drop the knife.

Make up your mind. Abraham cuts him free:
All that way for nothing.

My father did the same to me.
After school I longed to climb a tree.
But he held my hand
And at the bottom of the hill
He set me free.

The year comes to an end
Like a shutter in September.
Close the door on the new moon
And at the evening meal
Drink to the gift of life.

Mosquitoes come inside from cold,
Fragile letters on white walls
To mark the year's end.
Water the garden, for there's no frost yet
To melt in liquid on the flowers.

The spirit makes a full stop
When the New Year in Jerusalem begins.
Summer cool on every cheek turns suddenly to autumn,
And grates that smell of soot in England
Wait for the heat of winter,
And New Year to turn
Five more degrees upon the circle.

FIRE

Fire is always hungry –
As long as someone feeds:
It eats as if to melt the earth
And those who live on it.

All hunger threatens me,
And fire devours forests
More fiercely than the passion forests hide:
And fumigates pure heaven.

That's why I have a love for water,
A cool annihilating ocean
To devour the terrible devourer
And show the moon's white face in passing.

HIROSHIMA

You ask for a statement on Hiroshima.
All right:
If there's blood on the returning arrow
Bend the wind and suck

Till it becomes a flower.
Soldiers planted them among the rocks
And plucked chrysanthemums.

Who wanted peace before Hiroshima?
Mothers water soil with their tears,
And gardens thrive.

Don't let the Book of Memory close.
Stand among the flowers and read:
There will be no more ruins.

A statement on Hiroshima from me
Bleeds a peace
That brings more arrows.

SMALL AD

Fanatical non-smoking teetotal fruitarian,
Bearded, early fifties,
Good walker, plays chess –
But finding life dull,

Wants to meet big bosomed
Class conscious
Fox hunting
County-type carnivore female
With view to conversation
Or conversion.

WORK

Coming down first thing I see
The house in a lake of frost and mist,
Bare trees as in a battlefield
From which bodies have been moved.

By afternoon Life's all we've got,
No more over the horizon.
Mottled flame on a sure bed of coal
Burns out in the parlour grate,
Me at the desk creating lives:
No strength to break my own.

DEAD TREE

Say good things about the dead,
You'll never see them again.
That tree I just pulled down
Was dry from top to bottom.

Five years ago the taproots hissed
And a bullfinch sat on its highest twig
To eat the sky.
The tree drew clouds to climbing buds.

The brittle trunk snapped in two places,
Fell horizontal in the bracken
Broken by soil too thin,
And ivy fed off its over-reaching.

Say good things about that tree.
A young one near at ten feet high:
Bullfinch talons hold it down,
The poison kiss of ivy laps its base.

I scare one off and rip the other,
Drag the dead tree clear for winter wood,
Thinking good things about the dead
That only the blind of soul won't love.

SPRING IN THE LANGUEDOC

Rows of vines, cleaned up and tended
Like military graveyards in the north;
A magpie horseshoes back in guilty flight
Or at a yellow cartridge in the scrub.
A bee clings early to a flower
As if it might be last year's flame.
Warm grit under belly: a snake
Takes time to cross the sunny track.

Thyme and sage and olive died by winter
When they pledged undying love through storms and fevers
(Final and official when they said it)
Not knowing that undying love dies soonest.

WAKENING

A stiletto of light insidiosed
morning into the black room
pushed by a man stricken
with medieval pox
galvanized, Vitus-minded,
a jump-reaction to rip
the *paysage* like a painting into shreds
with halberded hands
when the shutters swing out.

A slight refraction of the haze
mars the hills and villages of dawn:
when I read the *Divine Comedy* at twenty
I didn't know that thirty years will
pass before my fingers turn the page
to nightingale and stonechat voices
plaiting their song
into an anthem of the Casentino.

On days of leaving
Flowers come
Rain holds back
Clouds give the sun a chance.

Driving away,
Blue sky fills the rearward mirror
Before a bend is turned.

Paradise draws off, a glint of flowers
Ahead, clouds like robbers gather
To discuss the lay-out of a forest.

Go in, trees starken:
The only land is Travel,
Recalling sun and flowers never met.

LIVING ALONE
(FOR THREE MONTHS)

When you live alone
No goldfish or canary to adorn
The baffle between room and sky;
When you live alone –
Reveille out of bed at the alarm:
A dim pantechnicon of dreams
Darkens up the cul-de-sac of sleeping
Suddenly a flower of smithereens;
Do ten-minute jumps so that the heart
Won't burst at running for a bus:
Bathe;
Set breakfast: appetite's topography
Of battlefield hurdles, to infiltrate
And leap the parapet to wideawake;
Dump supper et cetera;
Then do your day;
And when dusk threatens
A fresh skirmishing of dreams
You (like a soldier between campaigns)
Devise a meal before lights-out
And bivouac –

When you live like such –
The person that you are turns two
Divides into a body and a voice
One moment stentor and the other glib
(Morality contending: talks
To the stack of flesh that cannot speak)
But only to hear the voice's tune
Flagging words both ears must listen to:

On the activating of what's gone
The switching on from plasmic and bewitching times
Where you thought yourself in love but weren't
Or when you said: I love, but didn't
Or would, but couldn't:
But no denying love's starlined coordinates
Crossing the heart of positively did:
The onrush, the complete positioning
Of being in love, and loved,
When the one same voice and body sang
The breath of passion into memory,
Into death via love –
The faces, her face, the truth
Of love that lasts forever but could not:
Yet giving life along the way
Through mist's uncertainties
Because it was and did.

Living by yourself, you talk,
Reshaping the heart
To fill the empty spaces
Out of spaces that you one time filled,
Making the alone-day,
Breaking the day like a stone.

HOME

Landfall after the storm, going home through
White waves crumbling along the shore
Like piano keys pressed by invisible fingers,
Blue sky unfeeling what the sea does
To your boat, winds and subtle currents
Insidiously concerting.

Getting safe home through the storm
Provides no harbour or grandmother's face;
Waves turn you back as in a mirror breaking,
Each cliff falling on the soul
Like an animal with endless teeth.

PEARL

No wonder Job loved God.
He lived. God let him live,
Gave seven score years beyond his testing.

Job knew excoriations on his skin
Catastrophe dimmed one eye then the other.
He bounced words against God
But never despaired.
In gratitude God let him live
With friends and fatted kine
And fourteen thousand sheep.
God tested him, and let him live.

Pearl died without a Book,
Silent words flitting like dust
Till the dust inside her settled.
No winds could fan the dying fire into life,
She felt the dust settling,
Eyes from her wasted head saw the dust falling
And through the dust she saw me,
Cleared it with a smile to say goodbye.

LANCASTER

At twenty-two he was an older man,
Done sixty raids and dropped 500 tons on target
Or near enough. Come for a ride, son:
Hi-di-hi and ho-di-ho, war over and be going soon.
He opened a map and showed the side that mattered,
Thumbed a line from Syerston to Harwell.

Our bomber shouldered up the runway
Cut the silver Trent in May:
Three years in factories
Made a decade out of each twelve-month,
From the cockpit viewing Southwell Minster
Under a continent of candyfloss,
Fields wheatened green recalling
Chaff blown and remaining corn
To soften in my sweetheart's mouth,
Then into a hedge and crush the dockleaves into greensmear.

The pilot banked his hundred wingspan south:
How much magnetic, how much true, how much compass –
Work the variation through,
Two hundred miles an hour and a following wind,
Harder to get home again over lace of roads and lanes
Plus or minus deviation for a course to steer
Red and black on spread map at the navigator's table,
A smell for life of petrol, peardrops and rexine.
Run a pencil down from A to B –
Now on the fortieth anniversary I reinvigorate
The game which formed my life's dead reckoning
Impossible to fathom as in that bomber I assumed I could –

226

Everything mechanical and easy to work,
Map in top-left pocket, crawling the long coffin
Between bombracks and centre section
No view of the world for forty feet,
Parachute forgotten but who goes back
At seventeen? Who thinks the air is not for him,
Merlin engines all his own, strip map beckoning
Through Death's cathedral for a dwarf?
Everything is there to open: the rear gunner's turret
For a technicolor backward view
A track made good of woods and the botch of Leicester
Railways of Rugby, the sandstone of Oxford
The peace of Abingdon and first view of the Thames,
Canals and rivers of new reality, calico tablecloth
Hiding all in me, unseen from my chosen seat.

Better not to know how I reached the far-back turret
Of downdraught and upcurrents, eyes on the past's
Wide fan shaping my destination.
A button put me side-on to the slipstream,
An east-west variation of the view. People ignored
The buzzing of our passage, engines hiding the silence
Of a so-far buried life, looking over four guns
Ready to suck all spirits up like fishes to a net.

Cherish the distance between them and me
But get inside the theatre of what goes on,
Or open the door and tumble into space –
No one would know I'd gone or where, destroying
The homely panorama and my body.
Death would not burn the spirit but I'd be off
And out of the map, shoes, tunic and cap looted
By gravity: Hello! as I spin, so glad to know you
But I never will. There, I don't belong,
My place forever looking down and in.

Alone, far back, to face the vanishing horizon squarely on.
Dim as it is, don't go, corrupted by haze
Loving what I cannot reach. The theatre's anatomy
And madness missed, don't care about a full cast waiting
To come in order of appearance and perform their dreams,
Ambition's engine, curtains holding back
Till the planet Lancaster divides the space
And I return over empty bombracks to get born again.

Humanity is good to bait fish with,
Salt fish that dries in the throat
And needs vodka to turn it down.

Such human quality pressed
A jackboot onto his vocation.
A mob was set on him whose rage
Needed no stoking.

A writer has eyes, hands, a heart
A pen that sometimes scratches
Like a rose-thorn at a gardener's vein.
He borrows words

And lends them out at interest,
Turns from each season and
With no humility or ignorance
Tells a story to keep the world quiet.

DELACROIX'S 'LIBERTY GUIDING THE PEOPLE'

For the first few hundred yards
They knew her as a shirtmaker
Urging them over smoky corpses,
And when they said enough was enough
She climbed the lip of the barricade
To lead them over.

The world
Was impossible to open with a bayonet
That could not stop a cannon-ball in flight:
Nor could her red flag light them
Through a more than human darkness.

Then, whoever she was, she became LIBERTY.
No one knew when, by wonderful inspiration
She stripped off her shirt
And showed her bosom as a reminder
Of what brought them out of darkness.

Liberty, clothe your breasts
With that red flag –
I'll love you then.
Or let it guide the broken locomotive
Not the mob.

The boy with a pistol —
A cannon-ball took off his leg.
Your breasts gave liberty
But cured his worship.
Now he sells cheap pictures by the Louvre
Of *Mona Lisa* and *The Wreck of the Medusa*.

An Italian woman talking to her lover
On some far-off ocean
Mellifluously
From a villa in Liguria:
When are you coming back?
Shortwave static gruffed his voice.
I thought it would be soon, she said,
The scent of shrubs around her.

I love you, he said, but Neptune rules.
A sad laugh in her throat:
Yes, I understand,
So goodbye my handsome man,
I love you too.
The click of a telephone put down,
Sea noise rushing back.

Ah, love, I haven't lost you yet.
I love the sad laugh in her throat,
Face and body never to be seen
Nor flowers surrounding her.
I congratulate my rival,
And swing the needle onto other voices.

First of all
The brambles had to be pulled out
By the roots.

With thick gardening gloves
Against the spikes
I burrowed around the tree bole

And clasped them tight
And tugged their stomachs
Out of cosy soil.

It wasn't enough.
I had to walk away
Dragging the whole entanglement

From topmost branches,
Evergreen needles snowing me
As claws protested.

I got them down.
And yanked them loose
But it was slow work

Then cut away the ivy
Broke each brittle snake-branch
From sucker tracks

Halfway up and round the trunk,
Some fingers
More tenacious than an arm.

Next it was the nettles' turn
Them I grasped low down;
The taller they were

The easier they came,
Bunches of stings
Cast out to die.

Every parasite has its protection
Stings or prickles
Growing in alliance,

Making it difficult to start.
At last it's done:
The tree no longer burdened.

Space cleared:
The beauty of its trunk revealed:
The biggest anaconda of them all.

A tree with space
Grows ten years in two,
Breathing sky unhindered,

Vibrations
Running through both hands to say:
People need freedom like a tree.

NOAH'S ARK

(On 12 January 1987, at 2230GMT, I took down
an Italian news agency message in morse sent out
specially to ships. The text said that Noah's Ark was
no longer to be found on Mount Ararat, and gave
details. The report originated in Tokyo, and the
following lines are based on it.)

Earphones fed a message to the hand,
Hurried writing came through pat:
NOAH'S ARK IS NO LONGER FOUND ON MOUNT
   ARARAT.

Words in Italian, sparks of Aaron's Rod
Rained across the page in morse
Like intelligence from God:
NOAH'S ARK IS NOT FOUND ON MOUNT ARARAT.

Morse flowed like splintered glass
The text unfinished, rattling on:
BUT IN ALL PROBABILITY YOU WILL FIND NOAH'S
   ARK
ON A HILL FIVE HUNDRED METRES HIGH
ON THE BANKS OF THE TIGRIS BETWEEN SYRIA
   AND TURKEY.

Rome International Radio informed all ships
Swaying the emerald Atlantic waves
Urgent news of Ararat,
And Marconi operators wrote the gen

235

And typed it with the morning news,
Sailors with shocked eyes and lips atremble said:
L'ARCA DI NOÈ NON SI TROVA SUL MONTE ARARAT!

Perhaps Noah's Ark had been not lost
But one dark night dissected
And put on donkeys for a secret destination.
Hot-footed morse did not originate from God:
A Japanese expedition from an Electronics Firm
Led by YOSHIO KOU had combed
The scrub of Chaldees with a Bible and a map
Finally concluding that
NOAH'S ARK IS NO LONGER ON MOUNT ARARAT

Kids at school threw down their pens
Church and Synagogue were worried
And the Zurich bourse was flurried.
But fact and inspiration tell
How the Ark came on to Ararat because
The navigation of the Pilot was spot-on.
A dove and olive twig to guide the rudder:
And travelling all night above Lake Van
The snowy light was not one cloud of many
But glinting Araratic glaciers in the dawn.

Anchored by a terminal moraine
Noah ordered animals and humans to disperse.
God camouflaged the Ark from archaeologists
Who scour the land with lamp and map.
What YOSHIO KOU found by the Tigris
Was not an Ark but a canoe,
Though matters Biblical led him to state
NOAH'S ARK IS NO LONGER BEACHED ON ARARAT.

The story in the Bible's better:
Of how the Ark on Day Seventeen

236

After the flood that God begat
Bumped against the banks of Ararat.

The Ark, in spite of YOSHIO KOU, lies under rocks
On tufic Ararat, below a Turkish post
That looks on Persia.
I saw it in a dream, and sent a message back
By telegraphic key
Feet tapping to its rhythm on the mat:
NOAH'S ARK'S STILL HIDDEN ON MOUNT ARARAT.